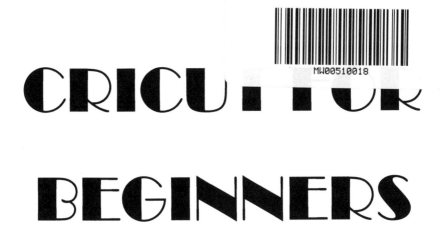

CRICUT FOR

BEGINNERS

The Ultimate Guide to Cricut Maker, tips and tricks.

3

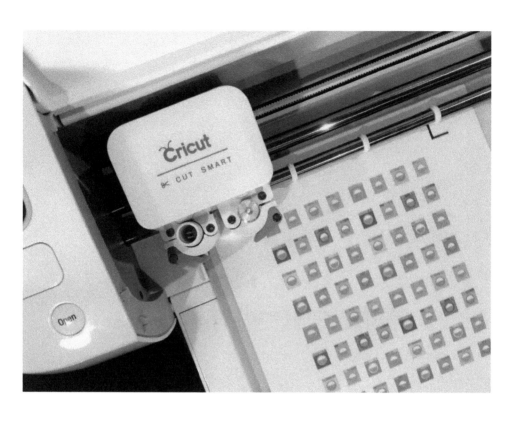

Table of Contents

CHAPTER 1

THE BASIC OF CRICUT MACHINE

The best cutting machines are Cricut machines

A Cricut machine does not need a computer interface. Cricut cutting machines are independent machines that produce patterns that are accurately cut from cardboard. These Cricut cutters are extremely popular with paper craftsmen and scrapbooking artists. Different models are selected by cartridges to allow scrapbookers and artists to create models in a selected theme. There are three different Cricut machines on the market. The most popular is the expression Cricut. Other models are the Cricut and the Cricut Create.

These machines all offer different cartridge designs, including recesses for the 50 United States and recesses for items with a wedding theme. The Cricut personal electronic cutter is usually supplied with the George cartridge. This cartridge offers a full range of basic fonts and shapes to help you on your way. Forms are purlin, shadow, silhouette, charm, split and sign. These shapes can be highlighted in 12 different sizes. The entire Cricut personal cutter usually costs around $

300. The Cricut Expression costs around $ 500 and uses the same cartridges as the Cricut personal electronic cutter. This machine can cut on a 12 "x24" mat. The larger cutting area makes it perfect for large format projects. The Cricut Create costs around $ 400.00 and is the same size as the original Cricut. When making Cricut, however, the cut shapes and letters

have a large format such as the expression Cricut. The "Don Juan" starter cartridge is usually supplied with this package. This cartridge offers various fonts, shapes, and creative functions. This cartridge contains shadow shapes, sewn, marked, surprised and under pressure. Scrapbook artists love Cricut machines because it is a great investment. With just one cartridge you can replace the need to buy alphabet-by-sheet alphabet stickers and shaped cutouts. With one cartridge you can design different looks in different sizes. By adapting to different paper sizes and choices, the Cricut machine can create different looks with one cartridge. One of the best features of a Cricut machine is its ease of use. School-aged children can use the Cricut machine for design projects or school reports. The cartridges generally offer around

250 worthies in 12 sizes. Moreover, Cricut offers many different cartridges. There is not much to do with a Cricut machine. They are perfect for scrapbooking, art, school projects and creating characters. The possibilities are endless with the Cricut machine.

It is a festive season

Christmas time means spending quality time with your loved ones. It is also one of those rare occasions that you show appreciation for them by buying Christmas gifts. It can only mean one thing: more money, more spending, more shopping. Shopping is not a problem for most women and some men, but with the hustle and bustle of the holidays looking for the perfect gift in mind for those close to you, it can be both challenging and stressful. But what if you want to save your extra money for the new year? Making do- it-yourself gifts will not only melt the hearts of your loved ones, but it will also show that hard work, not money, pays off. A Cricut machine is a perfect tool for making do-it-yourselfers. In short, a Cricut machine is used to cut paper and cardboard. But what makes it interesting is the multitude and variety of models that you can make with the circuit machine. One way to use the Cricut machine is to make homemade Christmas cards. You can help your children make your greeting cards. E-mails and text messages are so generic and impersonal these days. A handmade greeting card, especially something that you have done beautifully, will always show how much you care about your loved ones to turn it into a greeting card this Christmas period. Get inspired, be creative and build a personalized Christmas greeting card design that suits your mother, father, friend or best friend. The Cricut machine can be used to make do-it-yourself things for parties during the holidays. Party items, dresses, bridal items, and party bags can be more interesting and fun to look at using Cricut cutouts. Consider all the fun your children can have when cutting, gluing and designing party items for the holidays. It stimulates their sense of creativity, generosity, and appreciation for the holidays.

Definition of the Cricut personal electronic cutter and its use

When craftsmanship and scrapbooking become a passion for different styles, you cannot stray from authentic and beautifully designed materials that never go out of style. Today, artisans and users of Cricut are fearless and form spectacular and remarkable pieces with the help of modernized tools such as the Cricut personal electronic cutter. A personal electronic Cricut cutter is a type of Cricut machine with which you can cut shapes, letters, images, and words with one touch. Moreover, you do not need to use a counter, because this type of machine can be self-sufficient. You can use it for materials such as cardboard, parchment paper, vinyl, and any other cardboard or paper.

Cricut has many advantages and benefits. Some of them are:

1.   It is easy to use. No extra effort is required to complete your task in the production method, you only need access to the machine by clearly placing the material on the cutting mat and loading into the knife personal electronics, put the cartridge you want, choose your cutting style and press the "cut" button. Your best personalized and the personalized result will follow in this simple and simple way.

2.   It is practical and functional for everyone. Each of us has different skills and talents, therefore you will find this machine suitable

enough to be transported from one place to another. It only weighs 7 to 9 pounds and can be easily monitored and treated by one of your friends, especially for parties inside and out.

3.   It is very useful for crafting and scrapbooking. This machine can make paper crafts, scrapbooks, greeting cards and much more. It generally cuts more or less 1 inch to 5 ½ inches in height.

4.   It changes the contents of the cartridge is up to six unique ways. The cartridges contain hundreds and thousands of icons and artistic styles that can be used repeatedly. The good thing

about the personal electronic cutter is that it can adjust hundreds of variations and icons with a few pleasant methods.

5.   It offers a free start-up guide and user manual. For beginners and consumers like you, a user manual, a quick start guide, a power adapter, a knife construction, a 6 x 12-inch cutting mat, a file cabinet for a basic shape pattern, a manual every time you purchase one of these Cricut electronic cutting machines and a keyboard overlay

Cricut structure

Make this wall unique

You have just returned from work and went straight to your living room or bedroom to spend a relaxing time. You sit on a couch, without shoes, feet apart, and you notice that you look in a space. You then realize that your house or room does not feel like relieving part of the burden of your daily life.He looks dull, gray and every day. Perhaps it is high time to give this wall space a fresh and unique look. You can even create your artwork to fill your living space with a touch of creativity and design. If you are a Martha Stewart or Shabby chic, many crafts can help you get started with your wall project. The first is to choose your artistic medium. Are you planning to use paint or pastel on your artwork? Are you planning to use cut materials and custom designs, often used by people who love arts and crafts, such as scrapbooking? Are you planning to publish photos and make a collage or photo montage? It is better to choose a medium that matches the design of your room so that it is not moved. Choose the medium that you are most familiar with and choose a theme that interests you, so that you are motivated to start your wall project. Determine the size of the canvas. Most craft stores sell different sizes of canvas, and some have custom frames. It is better to consider the proportions of the size of your artistic project about the wall space that you are going to fill. You can experiment with different orientations of your artwork and what it will look like on your wall space. Make a plan when creating your illustrations. If you plan to use paint or pastel colors, choose an image - would it be an abstract work or a realistic representation of life? For beginners, it is best to try abstract pieces first because it gives you more leeway and allows your creativity to flow. For more structured designs you can use stencils to follow the designs on the canvas. If you plan to use cut pieces, you can use a Cricut machine.

Cricut expression - The most efficient cutting tool

The Cricut Expression uses comparable cartridges and knife blades and offers more flexibility. The compactness is capable of cutting designs that represent about half the structure of those that were originally made. It also offers various functions that are not available in the original, including the ability to change languages and units of measurement, can be used to cut in landscape mode, can be effectively used in multiple cuts for thicker materials, or even get mirror images with the flip function. The LCD screen is another of these functions that allow you to view the structure clearly before cutting. The disadvantages of the latter compared to the original are that it is larger and takes up more space on your table. If you occasionally go to places to work on projects, the latter is harder to wear. It is also much more expensive than its predecessor. Regardless of these facts, it offers much more versatility to your designs.

The ability to get a larger cut for the articles is ideal for creating banners and is particularly

useful for decorating bulletin boards or such large spaces. This article is great, especially for people who suffer from arthritis of the fingers or even for people with slightly shaky hands. Many artisans believe that the initial cost of the item is worth compared to the services it offers in the form of advanced designs. The price was initially quite high with a selling price of $ 499. Now the latter can easily be purchased for just $ 300. You don't have to be technically healthy to use this smart machine. You can easily connect it to a power outlet and start your project immediately. An optional toolkit can work very well.

Scrapbooking Cricut - Get to know this complex process

Everyone can appreciate what a great image can do for you. If you look at a beautiful photo that you took a few years ago when your child graduated, you will see what I mean. You look at this image and it looks like you have been teleported back in time and back in your child's graduation and you are starting to relive it. Images can say a million words and evoke an ocean full of emotions. Thanks to technology and everything related to it, we can now keep every special moment that we had, in the still mode or motion. Cricut scrapbooking also plays an important role. Scrapbooking has been around for a while and this is considered a very meticulous process. You see, people love making albums as an art and an elevated way to save images. Materials and images have been carefully selected to withstand the test of time. If you make a good album, it will probably last hundreds of years and even your fantastic album The grandchildren of the grandchildren will be able to see and relive every moment their grandparents lived. Is that not something Creating albums is made easier and faster thanks to the Cricut cutting machine. The Cricut cutting machine is a Cricut scrapbook tool that is responsible for cutting out the designs that you specify. When choosing the design for your album, you should always consider the theme. If the photos hosted by your album focus on a reunion that you and your family had, think of a design that will emphasize the theme. At the time, once the design was completed, the next challenge that you now face is how to create the design. Another tool that makes your work easier is the Cricut Design Studio. This bad boy is software with hundreds and hundreds of models that you can choose from. I guarantee that you can find everything about this software application. Another big advantage of this software is that it allows the user of the program to change the designs and even make new ones. Now technology is at its best.

Cricut products from Provo Craft contribute to the fun of scrapbooking

One of the best things about creating an album is to add decorations to your pages.

There are no rules about what you can and cannot use in your albums, apart from the size of your page. You have complete control over your project and can make decorations for your pages from any material you want, in any shape or size Paper is one of the most used materials for album decorations. Paper is readily available, inexpensive and comes in an almost endless variety of colors, structures and looks that can make your album something special. You can cut the paper into any shape and size for your album pages.

Why do scrapbookers choose Provo Craft Cricut?

First of all, because it is one of those elements that you can use to produce uniquely cut pieces of paper. If you have an album, you know how practical these tools can be. Why? Cutting paper in interesting

shapes and sizes is never easy. If you are new to this area, you often have to choose one of two options: get something with a nice outline that you can trace on a piece of paper and cut or do some simple tricks cutting of paper. Regarding the first option, this can take time. Regarding the second option, you must be skilled in using the tricks, otherwise, you will only get the poorly cut paper.There are many reasons to use Provo Craft Cricut products to cut paper for your scrapbook projects, such as:

Choice :there are many different models to choose from; There are simple and complex page border templates that can add a sophisticated decorative element to every page of your album. They also offer popular comic and television character forms such as Hannah Montana and forms that you can use for lettering. Cricut makes it easier than ever to add interesting designs to your album pages.

Easy to use : Even those who have never used them before will have no problems using the products. Why? You can cut paper considerably in no time in three simple steps. All you have to do is one; place paper, two; choose the design and three; press "Cut". That is it. So simple that even freshmen can do it

Consistent results : Provo Craft Cricut has specialized blades that can cut any type of paper, including vellum, so you always have the perfect cut With Cricut tools, creating album page decorations is easier than ever. Scrapbooking is supposed to be fun. Cutting paper doesn't have to be a job - if you have the right tool at your fingertips

Does the Making Memories Slice scrapbook cut machine cut it?

Scrapbooking is a wonderful form of art and memory preservation, practiced worldwide by young and old. Much complacency is obtained by scrapbookers who compile the pages of one or more photos, with a story, to preserve the memory of an event or to capture a unique moment.

Now everyone who does scrapbooking, especially with decorations, would be very familiar with the Making Memories company. They also make an amazingly wide range of incredible scrapbook tools, such as the label maker, the eye setter, the stamp set and much more.

The question is, with the popularity of scrapbooking cutting machines and the huge competition in the market from the two major cutting machine brands ... the electronics Provo Craft Cricut range of machines and the range of manually operated machines Sizzix, Can Making Memories can produce a cutting machine that is comparable to these two major brands?

Making Memories, which entered the Scrapbooking Die Cutting Machine market, only recently launched its Making Memories SLICE machine. The SLICE sells for $ 150.00 in the US, so it's half the price of the cheapest and slightly more expensive Cricut machine than the Sizzix Big Shot machine.

The SLICE cutter is marketed as the first cutting machine that does not require a power cord. It therefore really competes with the Cricut as an electronic cutting plotter and not with the Sizzix series of manual cutting machines.

Imagine being able to take him everywhere and show what he does without connecting him! Imagine the possibilities.

The Making Memories SLICE has features that are comparable to other electronic cutting machines on the market, such as being able to connect cartridges (called design cards) and cutting shapes and letters of different sizes. It does not have to be connected to a computer to work.

However, SLICE is trying to do something that the Cricut Personal machine does not do, namely cutting slightly thicker types of material.

The Cricut can only cut cards and the Sizzix can cut almost anything). However, the new Making Memories cutting machine cuts up to

0.5 mm thick. This means that you benefit from an electronic cutter, as well as the ability to cut a wider range of materials, which adds to the unique character of your album pages.

Since SLICE competes with Cricut and other electronic cutting machines, it is very well priced. It also takes up much less space than other electronic cutting machines. Of all reports, it also cuts very well and can cut leaves up to 0.5 mm thick.

One of the disadvantages of SLICE compared to the Cricut range is that you must hold the card during cutting because it does not have a sticky mat or other automatic cutting means. It takes some time compared to the Cricut that you can set and forget. However, for half the price, with the same benefits, including the bonus of missing a power cord, it is a major player in the punching machine market.

Scrapbooking - cutting and cutting machines

Cut-outs and scrapbooking machines make scrapbooking, card making and other paper-making fun and effective. The initial costs may seem daunting, but if you really love scrapbooking and do it often, it is worth investing in this type of scrapbooking equipment.

So what exactly is a cut?

The recesses look a bit like cookie cutters. He prints on different types of scrapbook paper and cuts perfect shapes every time with the help of a machine. The difference is to repeatedly cut small, complex pieces by hand or cut them in a second or two. They are an excellent time-saver. As one of the original embellishment options for scrapbooking, clippings can support any layout theme with shapes that celebrate most holidays, seasons, and occasions. With a little creativity and a few necessities, they evolve from simple forms to decorated masterpieces. Whether you make cutouts from cardboard, patterned paper or special paper, it is as simple as 1-2-3. Most machines work in the same way: you place cardboard or other material in a cutting block. You place the dice face down on the card. Then slide the cushion under the press and press the lever or button to cut the machine through the paper. There are also portable cut-outs that work just like a hole punch. Both come in different styles and shapes. Molds and their machines require an investment, so think about the functions of the machine you want before you invest. After you have purchased a machine, they usually only use the molds designed for them. The molds can be purchased separately or in packages. It is best to consider the type of scrapbooking layout that you intend to create and purchase.If you have been scrapbooking for a long time, you are probably bitten by the "I could use this I have to" beetle, just like a fisherman with

countless lures. If you are wise and only buy what you use, the investment is worth the time you save and the pleasure of being able to start pages at lightning speed! If you use different colors or different materials for your decorations, you can make unlimited combinations for your pages with only a few cutouts available. There are many machines on the market, but I strongly recommend the electronic machine Cricut Expression. They sell what they call cartridges, what their recesses are, and they have so many choices among you that you'll be amazed at the possibilities. They have Disney characters, cool font packages for intriguing letters for your album pages and all kinds of other thematic matrices. If you choose to invest, you can immediately produce accurate shapes from cardboard, patterned paper, special paper, and even thin metal sheets. You will find that you decorate carpets, newspapers and title blocks, while even their negative spaces created by placing recesses on larger recesses can serve as quick custom stencils or shaking frames You can cover the same cutouts with leafy pens such as fake metal charms, color them again with paint or ink, chain them or use them in shaker boxes - especially try the cutouts and scrapbooking machines!

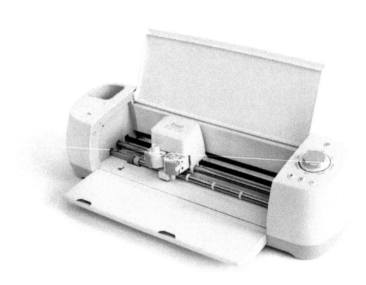

Start your scrapbooking machines with the new expression Cricut 2

Being a smart person has never been easier with the Cricut Expression 2. This practical device has made it easy and fun to make your craft projects unique and personal to your vision. Because the Cricut Expression 2 is not the first of its kind (hence the 2), the new elegant design and the color LCD touch screen with stylus show its growth over time. Let's face it, we not only want things to work well, but we also want it to be beautiful. Scrapbooking can become more of a creative outlet than a hobby with the many functions that Cricut Expression 2 has to offer. But make no mistake if you think you are limited to scrapbooking because you can use it for any creative project that you do or even add to projects that you have already done. With the Cricut the possibilities are endless, Unlike most new purchases you make, this tool comes with two cartridges that have already been loaded. The alphabet cartridge is what you will use for numbers, drawings and letters that bring everything you write to live. No more letters and numbers from Jane, because with the Cricut Expression 2 the simple is never an option. Now let's talk about the Essential cartridge. "Why?" can you ask? Well, let me tell you that this versatile cartridge is really where the creative fun begins! With this cartridge, you have access to countless designs, shapes, and artworks that will open your mind and let those creative juices flow so that the projects become the masterpieces you wanted. they are. Features such as the carpet preview so that you can see before you capture. There are also hardware settings, so you can adjust your work perfectly. You also have a cutting area light to help with the precise cuts that you need to make. There is certainly someone at the Cricut development office who wants to please the consumer,It always means a lot more when you or someone you love does something for you from nothing, because they have to put a lot of attention and energy into it to sit down and create it. With the Cricut Expression 2, anyone can open a new creative mode. Even if you have never used your inner cunning, you can use Expression 2 to expand your mind to the existing possibilities. And beauty is the freedom that you have while you can express yourself without the help of Hallmark or any other great manufacture. Imagine how refreshing it is to let yourself be who you are and to show yourself artistically using the expression Cricut 2. Sometimes we are so absorbed in our daily lives that we don't take the time to get out of its daily routine and do something that we can enjoy. So stop limiting yourself and start expressing yourself - have fun!

Overview of cutting machines - what you should pay attention to before you buys a personal cutting machine

To ensure that you get the most out of the cutting machines that you are investigating, you need to look for some attributes. This is mainly because many cutting machines can meet your needs. To begin with, the specific machine that you decide to purchase must be easy to use. By that I mean - you just have to insert the cartridge, make the right selection for your project and press Cut (or something similar). You can be sure that it is as simple as possible with the cutting machines. Secondly, the best cutters can do several things. You can make decorations for your home and a party. In the same way, it is possible to make scrapbooks, gift tags, labels, signs, and even school projects while using the cutter. Class decors, invitations and more also fall within the same discussed range. Third, look for a machine that can cut a multitude of different materials. From cardboard to vinyl to parchment, you don't want anything to escape from your cutter! You will be happy to see that many machines can handle the widest range of different materials. The thickness of the materials must be between ¼ of a an inch at the bottom to 23

½ inches at the top. Needless to say, this is a specification that is missing from most other strawberries, except the Cricut Expressions 290300. You want your cutter to accept all types of cartridges. This is especially nice for those of us who have many unused cartridges. Even if you do not have cartridges, you should know that the cutting machines that you purchase can accept any cartridge to ensure that you make the right decision. There are also these knives that come with new functions and modes. You can get a machine that happens to have 4 functions and 6 modes. They can also accept the horizontal and vertical orientation according to your needs. In short, you can be sure that whatever selection you make from the cutting machines you are looking at, it will certainly be of service. This is the main reason why most vendors of these machines do their best to give their customers a limited 1-year warranty. The implication here is that you can receive a new machine if the cutting machine that you purchase no longer works within a year of purchase.

Make your baby banner

Babies are always a source of joy and happiness. And having one in the family is fun and exciting. To make the welcome of the new baby more meaningful and memorable, a baby shower is organized. And in the case of a friend, he welcomes his sister-in-law's baby - his niece, You can make your baby banner the way he did. All you have to do is collect all the necessary materials, such as cardboard coasters, adhesives, pencils, and album pages. You can also add decorations such as ribbons, flowers, and strass to the list. Cutting materials such as scissors and cutters are also included. For adhesives, it depends on what you want to use, so it can be glue, paste or maybe even tape. It is not necessary to buy everything you need. Try to browse through your house and you will find most materials there. The next step in creating a baby banner is to decide which message it will contain. For example, you can say "Welcome baby" or "It's a baby girl" or "It's a baby boy". When you are done, you can now try to create a mental picture of how you would like to see it. Then start with the size, the pattern or maybe even the color of the banner. The color scheme may depend on the gender of the new baby. Usually pink means that it is a girl, while blue means that the baby is a boy. You can also use other colors if you do not want to stick to the usual. What is important is to use your creativity with this project. You can now start removing the letters from the message. Browse through your documents and choose the one that will do the best.

And when it's done, stick them directly on the roller coaster. The ultimate tip to do this is to be very neat while working on the project so that it looks nice in the end. You can even add glitter if you want, so this is worth considering. If you are satisfied with the appearance of things, it is done.

Scrapbook stickers to paste your photos

A scrapbook stock in every papercraft package must be sticky. More than one glue to be precise. The reason is that the adhesive adhesives differ from the old office tape or school glue. They have archive quality, which means that they will have to contain and protect your albums for many years to come. Always check your glue to make sure it is designed for scrapbooking, wear the quality of the archiver.

There are many types of adhesives and they also come in many different forms.

Wet glue is in the form of a "glue" in the form of a liquid past, a stick or a spray. A glue stick is a wet glue. Something like a modge podge is also a wet glue that can not only stick but can also change the appearance of a product. A wet glue in the form of a glue pin gives you precise and precise control over the glue. It's great when you write something that you plan to shine. Dry adhesives come in the form of adhesive tape, tabs, dots and photo corners.

Photo corners are placed on the outer edges of a project and never really stick the photo to the surface you work with. A tape drive is probably what you would work with if you chose to work with sticky photos or other decorations in your work. Ribbon runners come in all shapes and forms. They also release a repositionable and permanent adhesive. The slides can only be used once or you can purchase a tool and reload them with tape. The variety of available tapes is unlimited. Adhesive tape can cost between $ 1.50 and more than $ 15, depending on the size and capacity of the glue. There are also larger tape and glue machines that contain wet or dry self-adhesive cartridges. The principle behind these machines is to turn your scrapbooking product into a sticker. The machines vary in size to allow embellishments from 1 inch wide to a few centimeters wide. These machines can also adjust to different depths when it comes to turning your decorations into stickers. These machines also come with replaceable cartridges. Some of these machines also work with magnets and also work as laminating machines. The adhesives must be adapted to the material with which you work. For working with parchment paper or transparencies, for example, an adhesive is required that dries or comes in the form of transparent adhesive tape. If you want to add dimension to your projects, you can also work with pop-dots or a photo square supported by foam to add depth to the elements you work with. Whatever glue you use, make sure it is the right tool for the job. Make sure you know if you are working with a permanent or repositionable adhesive, as this can cause a costly mistake for your project. Also, make sure that the glue you use is of archival quality and acid-free. With all the effort you put into making your scrapbook projects beautiful, keep them in good condition and glued in place with scrapbook adhesives.

CHAPTER 2

HOW THE CRICUT MAKER WORKS

Configure your Cricut machine

Cricut projects - Ideas for light bulbs

The Cricut machine is a wonderful tool made by humanity. The world of scrapbooking has never been the same since the introduction of the Cricut cutting machine. This tool has revolutionized the way we cut patterns from paper, vinyl, and fabric. In the days of wood and metal, the art of preserving memories was primitive. Humans only used sculptures, paintings, and writings to record memories and ensure that future generations could see them. There was no way to record movement and voice at the time. Things have changed over the years. Technology has flourished thanks to the great minds that occupied the end of the 18th and 19th centuries. You look around and what was once a dream is now possible. A method or process that was introduced in the 19th century and that was considered a special way to preserve memories was the scrapbooking technique. This process involved making a book with images that had a common theme. When scrapbooking was relatively new, things were also difficult about the actual process of their creation. The concept formation was simple, but the cutting phase was what challenged the scrapbookers from far because the process only required the most stable hands on the planet. But with the introduction of the Cricut cutting machine, the cutting phase was very simple. There are many Cricut projects that you can involve when using your Cricut machine.

Let's talk about some, right?

There are Cricut projects that can help you gain personal satisfaction or generate income. Most people think that the Cricut machine is just a simple scrapbook tool. In reality, the Cricut cutting machine can be used for many things. Remember that the designs in your software tool or cartridges can be used for many things. To start, you can create greeting cards. I am pretty sure that we have all had unpleasant experiences in the past that have to do with not finding the right gift voucher. With a Cricut machine plus software or a cartridge, you can create your own personalized gift vouchers. You can sell them if you want or just keep making cards for your satisfaction. There are so many Cricut projects that you can use with the Cricut machine. The general rule is to be creative and not let your mindset limits.

How paper craftsmen import and cut SVG files for Cricut

With more and more paper artisans using digital clippings to create album pages, cards and decorations, the desire to learn how to import and cut SVG files on a Cricut digital cutting machine are also growing. Even starting scrapbooks do not have to feel intimidated by digital recesses. The process of

downloading, importing, preparing and cutting out designs is quite simple. And with two high-quality third-party software the market (Sure Cuts a Lot and Make the Cut), each with active notice boards and support forums, all problems must be solved easily. First of all, anyone who wants to use SVG files must have three things: a Cricut machine (either the original personal "Baby Bug", creation or compatible 12 x 12-inch expression), with a standard printer cable and Sure Cuts, cuts a lot. Sure Cuts a Lot (SCAL) and Make the Cut (MTC) are for sale at their respective manufacturers. SCAL is compatible with Mac and PC, while MTC is designed for PCs and only works with a Mac with Boot Camp or Parallels. Although some sites make files available, many sites are available for free. SVGs are available in all sorts of themes, from animals to vacations to toys. Many images are of comparable quality to the models available on Cricut cartridges sold by Provo Craft for $ 70 to $ 80 each. Once you find an SVG file that you like, download it to your computer. This is usually a simple process of clicking on a download button or link and then "decompressing" a compressed file by double-clicking on the name of the file once it is downloaded and then choosing extract. It is a good idea to organize your "collection" of SVG into folders by subject or through another system. If you use Sure Cuts a Lot, open the program and the mat screen will appear. You can set your virtual carpet to 12 by 12, 6 by 12 or 12 by 24, depending on the size of your Cricut machine and your actual carpet. Select "Import SVG" from the File menu and then navigate to the SVG image and click OK to import it. You can change the size of the image, rotate it and combine it with other images, among other functions. In Make the Cut, open the program so that the carpet screen appears and choose "Import" and then "SVG / SVGZ file". The image appears on your virtual carpet and you can choose "Shape Magic" and "Break" the SVG to separate it into the parts of the image. In both programs, as soon as the elements of the image are arranged as desired, usually place them in color and while maximizing paper usage, place your cards or your paper in the corresponding areas of the sticky Cricut mat. Save your project, make sure the Cricut carpet is loaded in the machine (check the pressure and speed of the knife) and then choose the "Cut" command. If you encounter problems, keep in mind that SCAL and MTC have active support communities.Another advantage of using third-party software with Cricut is the ability to cut almost any True Type font, including soldering (assembling) letters. After the design is cut, it can be assembled with glue. Many paper artisans, as well as those who use SVG designs for school projects, home decor or other uses, would like to add dimension and add their creativity with white gel pens, chalk, ink, glitter or dimensional "pop" dots. Like many paper artisans who like to save money while expanding their creative options, the use of designer-cut files with a cutter such as Cricut is an easy process to control, thanks to high-quality SVGs and third-party software.

Another idea a dollhouse card with the Cricut Wild Card cartridge for a Cricut card - Make

How about using the Wild Card Cricut cartridge with your Cricut Expression machine and making a personalized handmade greeting card exactly as you imagine it. You must like the Cricut Expression machine. I had to make a birthday card for my niece. I knew she was making a dollhouse with her mother, so I wanted to make this handmade greeting card special. After I discovered her colors that hurt the dollhouse, I decided to use the same colors for the handmade card. The use of my Cricut Expression and the Cricut Wild Card cartridge was the perfect choice for my Cricut card idea. All the samples showed that this Wild Card Cricut cartridge was used for the relocation/change of address, but I decided to make it into a dollhouse. I set up my Cricut expression to cut the card into 7 "and it was a big size

because I wanted to decorate this greeting card by hand with a nice card and scrapbooking decorations that I have. I used a pink rhinestone for the door handle, I had a 3D EK Success sticker from a white fence that I cut to size and also funny palm stickers to accentuate the front door. I finished it with a

3D pink butterfly sticker from EK Success. For the interior, I have all the rubber stamps that I have scanned (and that are many stamps, it is a good thing that I have organized my rubber stamp stuff in containers that are labeled), but I decided to hand the inside of this greeting card very easy to make and just use a rubber stamp that says a happy birthday.

Your do-it-yourself wedding

Most women dream of a big marriage because they were little girls. They dream of a very large ballroom in front of the reception, an expensive dress with intricate designs to wear and many guests who would attend the special event. However, some women are on the practical side. They are the ones who prefer a simple and calm but nice wedding, outside of what is stereotyped in wedding magazines. If you want to get away from the stereotype, you need to prepare, because it would be a big challenge to have a do- it-yourself wedding. Most organizers can help, but if you have a limited budget, who needs a wedding planner? So you have to organize your priorities when setting up this marriage. First, you have to decide where you want your wedding to take place. Is it in a church, in a garden, on the beach, or is it somewhere near or far away? If you prefer somewhere, a destination wedding with a limited budget is for you. Then you must determine the general mood of your marriage. Do you find it classical or magical, or do you want it to be noisy and full of festivities? If you choose the latter, find a place that meets your needs and prepare the music too! If you want to dance, then certainly! Just make sure you can party in your house until dawn. If you try to google a place, you will notice that there are many options available to you. However, you must limit your choices. You must consider the cost of the place because of your budget, and you must also consider their catering service and other hotel accommodations. It also depends on the opening of these places for DIY weddings, because some may not be flexible enough with their accommodation. If you've already found the best place, the next thing to do is eat, music, and other necessities. Make sure you stick to your budget and do not make unnecessary adjustments. Where possible, negotiate. It is better to buy something under your original budget than to go overboard.

Make sure you organize your priorities and make a list for them, as this would make your job easier. In this way, you would not be lost and you would not forget anything. Moreover, you would also have an idea of your performance. After all, you are not the only person who has to work for this marriage. You have your family and friends to help you. Don't be afraid to ask for help. It is your marriage and you have the privilege of asking a favor from anyone who wants to become a volunteer. You can ask for a small favor, such as having Cricut information for your gifts or to pick up the Cricut Expression machine that you bought at a local store into something great, such as making crafts for your wedding gifts.

Make great headlines for scrapbooking

Your album layouts can be significantly improved by finding titles that attract attention. A good way to do this is to start with an abundance of alphabets with scrapbooking. Since many of us are not satisfied with our writing and we are always looking for alternatives, here are some that make a good start.

First, how do you place your words on your page?

The easiest way is to find a writing style that you like and practice until you are satisfied. Otherwise, it is a trip to your local album store to spend your hard-earned money on alphabets - again! So ... after loading the dishwasher, washer, and dryer, taking the children to school, making appointments for the dentist and the hairdresser for everyone, attending the meeting at the PTA and getting the groceries for dinner, you just have time between your date with my husband and pick up the dry cleaner to run to the scrapbook store before it's time to pick up the kids from school, give them a snack, prepare dinner so it's all ready when you all come back from football, then at home to eat, help with homework, bring the kids to bed and discuss some family issues with my husband before I hit the bag myself ... By the way, when do you have time to scrapbook?

Anyway, if you go to the scrapbook store, what will you find there? You should find a huge selection of

- alphabet stickers

- rub-on

- cuts

- stamps

- word and sentence decorations

Each of them can create headlines, newspapers, and feelings in your layouts.

Let's see a few of them ...

Alphabet stickers

These come in all shapes, sizes, colors, fonts and materials - cardboard, bubbles, jelly, pebbles, to name just a few. They are very easy to use and add fun and color to your scrapbooking layouts. The disadvantage is that they never seem to contain enough letters and that you can only create a few words in the same style. However, you can use remaining letters as "upper case" at the beginning of paragraphs in your journal. In this way you can get away with different styles. And with some layouts you can, for example, mix and match different styles in the title or bullets. It is also nice to add characters in random style in the middle of your diary.

Rub-ons

They were called transfers when I was a kid, and these are just letters. They now come in the form of individual letters or words and sentences in black or in different colors, as well as many beautiful designs. As the name suggests, you can simply rub them on your page with the included stick. (You can

use a bone file or piece if you lose the stick.) It is a good idea to cut the words you want to use and place them carefully, or you can find single pieces of the word that you didn't want. transfer.

The rub-ons look good and give a professional finish.

Alphabet stamps

It's a good buy because you can prevent the "never-need-all-letters-I-need" syndrome that occurs with other media - and they are reusable It is easy to stamp words with double letters if you choose clear stamps. Place the letters on a clear acrylic block to form your word, leaving the correct space for the double letters that you add with a second pass. To keep the correct opening, place another stamp where the double letter goes and when the word is ready, remove it and leave a space where you will stamp the missing letter later. You can stamp letters precisely because you can see where you are stamping. After use you simply wipe them back on the sheet and they are ready for the next time!

Other ornaments of the alphabet

There are chipboard letters, metal letters, perforated letters, self-adhesive letters, button letters, brad letters, Scrabble letters, paper tile letters; alphabets in countless colors, materials, and bling ... you name it, you can probably get it! You will find many interesting accents to try on your scrapbook pages.

Mechanical and electronic systems

The different cutting machine systems have beautiful alphabets, but if you are not yet familiar with scrapbooking, they may seem like an expensive way to make your heads. The results are excellent and worth it if you think you will also use some of the many other forms available. You will use it a lot, especially if you make your greeting cards. Some names to watch out for are Sizzix, Big Shot, Quickutz, Cricut and Xyron, just to name a few. You can even buy a set of alphabet stamps.

What remains?

But before you go to your local scrapbooking store, consider using your computer. You already have several fonts and there are many more that you can download for free from the internet. Your computer is one of the most versatile ways to make a headline or journal. With the huge selection of fonts available, you'll find one that fits your layout design, but size flexibility is even more useful. You can have the font as large as you want for a title, or small enough to get all your journaling on a tag. You save a lot of money using your computer.

How do you get titles from your computer in your layout?

It is very easy and quick to do.

- Choose a font and the correct size for your project.

- Type your words and then print with the reverse image setting on your printer options.

- Go to the wrong side of the selected design or paper or cardboard,

- Cut and respect your project or your scrapbook card.

- If you cannot or cannot find the setting for the reverse image:

- follow your words carefully - a lightbox helps you here - on the right side of the paper,

- cut into your lines.

And voila.

It's great to have so many types of alphabets for our layouts. However, do not try to use one style too often, as it is monotonous to create and view an album full of the same designs. Now you see how easy it is to make great titles and journals, nothing stops you. Have fun making your memories - and may you have time to save them in beautiful scrapbook page layouts.

Get some spirit back in art and craft

Wow! Do you love Arts and Crafts? Have you heard about the Cricut expression? If you didn't do that, you slept under a rock. This machine is great. It is a cutting plotter that can make large amounts of amazing designs in different sizes and it comes with thematic cartridges that you can purchase depending on the type of project you are working on. So if, for example, you are working on a project to decorate a young child's room, you can get a cartridge with predefined shapes that you can easily connect to the Cricut Expression machine and set the desired amount and size of recesses. The machine will then shape any design and produce clippings with thousands of different shapes and designs of your child's most loved cartoon characters that you can use to decorate your child's room. The cartridges come in hundreds of different themes, such as "Storybook", "Joys of Season" and "Animal Kingdom." So you can use the Cricut expression for many different types of projects. You can create hundreds of your own

Christmas greeting cards at the touch of a button or you can create beautiful seasonal shapes to paste into a scrapbook. You can use it to make decorations for a party or Thanksgiving and Halloween and the best thing is that you don't even need a computer. The cartridges are connected directly to the machine itself. So you can now buy one machine and several cartridges that you can use for different projectsThe Cricut Expression and the Cricut Cartridges are a valuable addition to your home. Consider the money you spend on buying in-store generic decorations for each event. Now you don't have to do that anymore. You can make one yourself and also involve your children in creativity.

More than 50 ways to make scrapbooking easier

1.   You do not have to write a book in your diary (no pun intended). Are you running out of time? Just record names and dates. How about adding a short descriptive description, say "Swimming on Candlewood Lake".

2.   Mat your photos. You do not need any decorations to embellish your pages. Just add a brightly colored or assorted color blanket behind your photo. But beware, too many mats make your page too busy and overloaded.

3.   Use kits. Most kits come with everything you need to make a great album. They are usually related to the theme.

4.　　Use pre-designed albums. These are perfect for those of you who just don't have the time. Ideal for giving gifts.

5.　　Steal a layout idea from a friend (I'm sure it would be honored) or online.

6.　　Save time by organizing a "cropping session" for the television one evening, so if you go to the scrapbook, it's already done! TIP for cropping: cut everything that is not relevant (do you need this stranger in the background?).

7.　　Organize your photos. This time organize a "Organize your photos" session for the television. Organize them by date, season, and event.

8. Fixed? Choose a POPS color from your photo and use it as the color theme for your layout.

9. Have all your supplies handy. That way, when you are ready to continue, you are ready. No more "where did I put those damn scissors!"

10. Organize (see # 9)! Make sure that part of your house (office, bedroom, closet ...) is dedicated to scrapbooking and organize so that everything is easy to find. Label your drawers, use shoe boxes for your smaller supplies, you get the picture.

11. Use patterned paper as the background for your layout. This removes the guesswork about how you will design your page. Paste a few photos and you're done!

12. Use a stamp to add a little spice. It is just as fast as drilling a hole! You can also add a bit of style to the corners of your photos this way.

13. Cut a piece of paper with a pattern, such as a flower, and use it as a cutout on your page.

14. Take album paper and a paper cutter and cut out the corners. Paste them on your album page for quick design.

15. Tear off scrapbook paper to give your layout dimension. You can use your hands or buy cheap edges to help you with this work.

16. Good old-style stickers add a lot of depth and creativity to your pages.

17. Paste your photos diagonally on your page for an interesting look.

18.   You do not have to give all your pages a title. A small newspaper can be anything you need.

19.   Oops! You messed up your newspaper ... we've all been there. Quick solution: cut a square paper to cover your mistake and voila - you just have another chance!

20.   Use as few supplies as possible, this way you will not be overwhelmed (album, paper, stickers, pens, adhesives, scissors and of course photos, are all you need to get started)!

21.   Are you too busy with your big family vacation? Add a transparent bag to the back of your album cover and save it there. Make sure it does not contain any acid.

22.   Use thick foam adhesives to paste your photos to add dimension.

23. Simply choose 1 to 3 photos that fit on a page. Too many matches, too many people. Keep the rest of the images in an acid-free photo box.

24. Format your page before you begin. Decide what it will look like and if you cannot put it in an album right away, then archive what you will use in a folder or page planner.

25. No stress. Your layouts do not have to be developed. The most important thing is that your photos are safely placed in an acid-free album.

26. Too many photos for an event? Eliminate them and eliminate blurry, unnecessary and distracting images. It can be stressful to think that you should use ALL the photos that you have taken if you do not take them.

27. Use cutouts. There are very nice cutting machines, such as the Cricut and Epic 6. The cuts will dress stress-free!

28. Use a journaling label. This will make your layout fun and reduce the stress on how to title your page.

29. Use a simple layout plan for your album. By this we always mean the same layout, making it different by changing the color scheme on each page. Consider how quickly your album is ready!

30. Use stencils and color them with chalk, pencil or marker. I know it sounds a lot of work, but it isn't. Place the template (on paper or directly on your page) and draw on it! Now you have added a nice handmade item to your

layout that looks like you spend a lot of time on it.

31.   Get help! Get help from your daughter or even your husband. You not only spend quality time with your loved ones, but you add a different style to your album.

32.   Souvenirs add great decoration to your layouts. Tickets for a Rolling Stones concert and a photo or two are enough!

33.   Don't have the time or the will to scrapbook your life? Choose important events such as your child's marriage, childbirth, and first communion. It is well!

34.   Little inspiration? Join a scrapbooking forum to get ideas from other scrappers!

35. Rub-on is easy to use and looks great. All you need is a popsicle stick to scrub them and you're ready to go!

36. Books, books, books! Go to the library or visit your local bookstore for scrapbooking or quote books. I love the quote books, they are great for titles!

37. Decorate your pages with borders. You can use sticker borders or make a quick border with paper. You can tear the edges or use a border template and cut it out.

38. Spend an hour watching Desperate Housewives making boundaries. Cut the paper into strips, create the scalloped, wavy, zigzag edges using a border template, or you can tear the edges by hand. Add stickers for the pit. Now you are ready to go the next time you get rid of it.

39. Do you not have any stencils or templates to hand? Look around ... use cool objects in your house to use as stencils!

40. Not sure which glue to use? I know ... the options are endless. Whatever you choose, stick to adhesives that are specifically designed for scrapbooking and do not use non-acid glue. I love the tape drive. It is EASY to apply and a little goes a long way!

41. Use scissors with a decorative border for more fun! Cut out a photo, paper, and mats.

42. Become a member of a scrapbooking club or create one yourself! Organize a harvest and scrap. Share your ideas and tools. You would not believe how much you can do in these types of settings!

43. Tracing paper for an extra dimension. Why only have one mat under your photo if

you can double or triple it? Combine the solids with patterned paper for an extra feeling!

44.   It is overwhelming to think of everything you can do with a layout or what you should do. Start with a focal point and accessorize from there.

45.   Set goals. Make some time off every week for scrapbooking and do it (you know, sports fun but only more fun) !!! It doesn't have to be a huge amount of time. Maybe an hour or two here and there. Eventually you get caught.

46.   Use tape to perforate your pages. Add a bow or border to your layout. It is as simple as sticking on.

47.   I can't emphasize this enough ... don't think too much about what you're going to do! Believe me, I was someone who spent an hour thinking I had to do the best layout of all time. What a waste of time, not to mention the frustration that comes with it. Just stick to a plan and go for it.

48.   The embellishments add a little spice. If you like the look of the decorations, use them! They look difficult and some of them are, but if you stick to the basic decorations such as buttons or brads, they can be a quick solution to a page dilemma.

49.   Don't lose everything. If you have photos that you like but don't have the space or energy, organize them in an acid-free photo box.

50. Keep a small notebook with you. If you are inspired or have a great idea, write it down! It will be extremely useful when you sit down for scrapbooking.

51. Take a deep breath and do not stress. Scrapbooking is supposed to be fun, so don't let it raise your blood pressure. Don't take it too seriously, just bring your photos down!

52. If all else fails, hire a company that will actually do your scrapbooking for you. It can be expensive, but at least it will be!

Chapter 3

EVERYTHING YOU NEED TO KNOW ABOUT DESIGN SPACE

Everything you need to know about storage space

Storage space is an essential and vital feature of any home, especially if it is smaller and more than one person lives at the same time. You need to find ways, such as drawers under the bed, to use any small storage space you have. There are many ways to do this, and you can even install short drawers under the bed in your closet for that extra increase in space that you thought was fully utilized. As I said, there are many ways to bring this storage enhancement to your home and I agree that the cheapest way is to do it yourself, but if you want to do it right, you better hire a professional that can offer up to 50% more storage space from practically nothing, or at least that you thought was nothing. Both methods work, but at least the most effective method is to seek professional advice.Yes, there are storage professionals under the bed because as stupid as it seems, finding storage space is not as easy as you think and you need to know a few things about this type of activity to make the best of it. Interior decorators, we'll call them that, can help a lot in this industry and they don't even demand much. For some storage tips, they charge around $ 10 per hour, so ask as many questions as possible. You can even ask the interior designer to buy all the necessary equipment and also install it if you don't have the time. In this way, you ensure that the work is carried out properly and you can take advantage of the extra storage space that you have with the deal. Some people say that the drawers under the bed are worth much more than you pay for some drawers and cupboards, so I would agree with them if they come out and hire someone to do the job. storage for them.

What makes a modern kitchen?

A so-called "modern" kitchen will always have a balance between functionality and aesthetics. However, each owner can apply his expression when incorporating new and interesting materials and products. Therefore, the designs seem to vary from house to house and from year to year, even though the underlying basic concept remains the same. A homeowner can adopt a modern theme by installing frameless European style cabinets with horizontally aligned functions and recessed handles. Another owner can also create a modern theme by transforming traditional cabinets with modern materials and finishes. Both options improve the functionality and aesthetic appearance of a kitchen.

Requirements for kitchen design

Whatever the theme, every kitchen must have specific design features. These are standard requirements that apply universally to all cooking areas. That is why you must ensure that your modern kitchen also meets these requirements. The three Australian standards that apply to all kitchens are: AS 1428.1, AS 4299 and AS 1428.2.

According to the applicable standards, your kitchen must have the following main characteristics:

Sufficient space that allows free and free movement in the cooking space. Sufficient storage and working surfaces mounted at easily accessible heights. Appropriate devices with user-friendly buttons, controls, and handles.

Easily accessible facilities for waste disposal.

Adapted to the changing needs of all users and future changes.

Comparison of modern and traditional kitchens

To better understand what the modern theme entails, you must compare it with traditional themes. These two themes have so many contrasting features. Although it is described as "traditional", this theme has not gone out of style. Traditional kitchens give an intimate and warm feeling, as well as a touch of comfort. This theme fills your kitchen with the timeless ambiance that is characteristic of rural chalets. In contrast to traditional themes, the modern look gives a chic and trendy feel. This theme is not only fashionable but also very effective. In contrast to the curves and organic forms embodied by traditional kitchens, a modern theme presents elegant block shapes and clean, straight lines.

Main features of the modern look

The specific characteristics remain unchanged, regardless of the materials and products that people install in modern formats. One of these functions is the functional map. This map deviates radically from the traditional work triangle. The floor plan in modern themes is built around your lifestyle situation. It is designed as a personalized plan that not only focuses on functionality but also offers the highest possible comfort. The seamless fixtures are another important feature of modern fixtures. Such a kitchen would have matching devices that display a well-coordinated appearance. The devices tend to have an elegant and modern look. Moreover, homogeneous uniformity is achieved by integrating the devices into the cabinets. Such designs even go so far as to create the impression of a single solid piece with integrated devices.

Everything you need to know about installing a horse stable

When it comes to building a horse barn, you need to know what you are doing. Not only will the comfort of your horses depend on it, but also their health. Health and comfort are directly influenced by the way you build and maintain your stability. That said, a good horse shed should not cost you an arm and a leg, but a bad shed could cost you your horse. Read on to find out everything about building a horse barn. Location - The first thing to consider before building a horse barn is the location. Not only does the location affect your animals, but it can also affect the infrastructure of your barn. When you plan to build your horse stable, you must avoid the low valleys. If you build your stable at the foot of a hill or in a valley, you run the risk of flooding. Rain, drainage and melted snow can damage your infrastructure and endanger your animals. When choosing the location, you must build your shed against the wind of your house or other buildings. This prevents the fumes from the barn from disturbing you at home. Barn layout - spend time designing your barn and think about where to build storage and office space. A good rule of thumb is to place desks, bathrooms and storage space in the middle of your shed. This allows you

to seal the center so that you can heat or cool the room without heat or cool the entire shed. Don't forget to overfill storage or office space, unused food or supplies can be damaged or rot, plan accordingly. If you do not want to take care of the interior of your barn, you can order a kit for horse stables online. Boxes - The design of your horseboxes is very important, so although you don't want the box to be too small, you also don't want it to be too spacious. A small stable is unhealthy for your horse, but a large stable can be annoying to clean and maintain. A good rule of thumb is to keep the stable at 12 square feet, which gives the horse enough space to move around without sacrificing valuable space. Ensure adequate ventilation through the stables. Ventilation - Ventilation is crucial and is perhaps one of the most important parts of your shed. You cannot train your horses in the barn; they will poop where they are going. Make sure you always have good ventilation to reduce the smell and prevent your pets from getting sick. Keep both sides of your shed open at all times to increase airflow.

Everything you need to know about S.E.O. But where I am afraid to believe

Perhaps you have your own business or you are a critical cog in the company machine that is responsible for marketing your company, brand, product or service. If that describes you, here are eighteen things you need to know about web marketing but were afraid to believe.

1. It's time to be heard.

Your mother told you that "children should be seen and not heard," but that you are no longer a child. So why listen to all those guys who tell you not to use audio on your website. If you want to provide content that people will remember, try to make your site speak.

2. Nothing beats the real thing.

In a world where everything is virtual, nothing beats the real thing. The sound and image of real people who convey your marketing message make it a credible and memorable presentation.

3. Unlock the classic straitjacket.

Generating traffic to your site is great if those visitors stay long enough to figure out why they should do business with you. If your website traffic leaves as fast as it arrives, search engine optimization may not be the answer you were looking for.

4.   Link your way to the dark.

Do you know the mutual linking strategy that everyone is talking about to generate leads? Have you ever thought that every link to another website is an invitation to leave your site? Is this really what you want - invite people to leave? I do not think so!

5.   The voice of your company is his personality.

Give your business a professional voice, with a sophisticated script from a professional voice-over announcer that presents an engaging and memorable marketing message and a unique brand personality. Or do it yourself and sound like an amateur. The choice is yours.

6.   Address priorities in reverse order.

If your web design company distorts your marketing message to meet the technical technology of the day that only looks good in a popular browser, you have hired the wrong guys. It is not a matter of technology; it's a matter of communication.

7.   Text ads are dead. Live web video.

Shrinking your marketing message to a pay-per-click text ad is the same as trying to attract potential customers using one of those real estate newspaper ads where every word needs to be decoded. Start communicating with a web video that tells a story - your story.

8.   No one has ever bothered anyone to buy.

The vast majority of the website text is boring, unimaginative and self-promotion. If you don't present a fascinating, focused story, you just waste people's time. Seduce your audience with an informative, entertaining and memorable presentation made by marketing professionals.

9.   Too many good things are not so good.

Concerned about loading times and search engine optimization, so you've emptied most of your images and media files and put enough text on your site, which would take a month to study; but did you think if someone read this? And that is assuming that people in the first place could never find what they were looking for.

10. Stop hiding behind your email address.

You have a great website. He tells visitors everything. They only have to place an order. But wait ... someone has a question. So they go to your contact page and look for an e-mail address. No contact name. No address or telephone number. You have provided a Q&A, FAQ and a list of technical specifications. What else do they want? Well, what they want is to talk to someone to make sure you are legitimate and if they have a problem, you will lag what you are selling. Idiot.

11. Do you suffer from superfluous redundant reflux?

Search engines are fond of content. They index all your text in search of keywords and phrases. So what are you doing You repeat and repeat things over and over again to make sure the search engines understand what you are. It is a shame that all your web visitors are destitute by reading your excess copy and leaving because they have forgotten why they were there.

12. Inform. Light up. Persuader.

Knowledge is today's high-quality product. If you have skills that people want to learn, then you have to sell something: something to build a business. But if you don't know how to present this knowledge to an audience, your skills are unsaleable. If you want to get paid for what you know, you better know how to get your content there.

13. It is not a matter of numbers; It is a matter of quality.

It is not about how many visits you get to your website, but how long visitors stay on your site and how much information they keep after they have left. It is about the quality of traffic, not quantity. And the best way to generate quality traffic is to provide content that is easy to find, understand, and remember.

14.   Don't play Constant S.E.O. Catch up.

When an S.E.O. whizz kid finds a trick to beat search engine algorithms, search engines change their criteria. This means that you constantly have S.E.O. plays. to catch up. Good for the child, not so good for you. And have you ever wondered how all these search engine optimizers can guarantee you and everyone else selling them the best billing - a little hard to believe, right?

15. Show me what to do.

Anyone who has ever spent the night before Christmas deciphering the obscure instructions from the manufacturer of the bike you bought for your child or the bizarre images that came with the do-it- yourself the kitchen that you bought from 'you know who', knows that there is nothing like a good video to explain how part A fits part B

16. Even cows have marks.

If you have a business, you have a brand. We are not just talking about a logo. We talk about everything you do: your website, your printed matter, everything, including how you answer the phone. You pick up the phone, right? If your web design company doesn't understand if they don't create a brand personality, what do they do?

17. Lost In Space.

Go to one of these impossible to navigate websites. Perhaps the navigation system is not working in your favorite browser, or perhaps the navigation system is so confusing that visitors get lost in the hell of cyber content. Information architecture, how people find the content they are looking for, is essential to creating a satisfying user experience.

18. You can have it in two ways.

Do you remember that your mother told you that you couldn't have dessert if you didn't have your broccoli? It sounds like these search engine gurus who can tell you everything that you can't have multimedia on your site. Well, you're a big boy now, and if you want this hot fudge multimedia sundae, you can have it. And you can also have all copies that are suitable for search engines. Who says you can't play both?

Everything you need to know about designing south-facing houses

It is believed that a south-facing house gives you a relaxed and financially secure feeling. When designing this house, make sure that the door is in the south or the 4th Pada in the south direction. The reason is that there is a strong belief that when the door is facing south, this is a good sign. You must ensure that the main bedroom and the hanging tank are in the southwest corner. When designing the master bedroom, be careful not to compromise the design space for the facade. You must leave enough free space on the east and north sides. You must avoid leaving much room in the south because this is a sign of bad things. You should also avoid building a septic tank, well, garden or porch in the southwest direction. Some of the best things to build in a southwestern direction are the office or the store. Placing the two in this direction is a sign that you will flourish and improve your financial situation as a homeowner. When designing the store or office, ensure that the south wall is much higher than the north wall. It is to get better results.

1. Regarding the septic tank, you must build it on the north side of your house. To prevent contamination, ensure that the septic tank is 15 feet from the crankcase or borehole.

2. To prevent breakdown, the stairs must point to the south, west, southeast or northwest corner of your home. It should never be in the northeast corner of the house.

3. More things to do

4. If you have not yet bought a country, you must buy one that goes from south to north. If

you do not know the directions to the area, ask your architect for help.

5.   You must find the kitchen in the southeast or northwest corner. You must look east or west while cooking.

6.   If you like a garden, you must place it in the southwest corner. You can plant trees in this direction, but you must ensure that they are not too high to cover your house.

7.   conclusion

8.   As you have seen, there are many tips to take into account when designing a south-facing house. To get ideal results, you must work with a certified and experienced architect.

The Panasonic SC-HC30 compact stereo system and everything you need to know about it

The compact is what everyone now wants in every device they buy. No big devices - that's the trend. Unless you get a 41-inch LCD TV, you can make it smaller. But the quality cannot be compromised by the small size, such as the compact Panasonic SC-HC30 stereo system that is small, but certainly terrible, in a good way. I would like to share everything about this model with you.

design

It is compact as it is and extremely thin. It makes it easier to make room when you get home with this thing in your arms. With dimensions of 4 " x 19.6 " x 7.9 " inches and a simple weight of 6.2 pounds, you can easily take it anywhere and transfer it to any room. at home at any time. It is also very nice to watch because of its elegant design. It has motorized sliding doors that keeps the iPod docking station and the LCD screen out of sight, and admire the mechanism when it is opened. It is easy to make room for this device and it is also easy to hold it in place as long as the front part stays open, so when you need to dock or disconnect your iPod or iPhone and load or remove your CD, you do not have to move the device over and over again.

video

The fluorescent screen makes it easy to see the necessary information about the song being played, the tracking number on the CD, the duration of the song, the artist name, the album name, and more basic information. The screen also goes dark when not in use and the automatic shut-off function switches the device off after a while when it is not in use.

audio

The speakers of this device are passive dual radiators that use advanced bamboo cones that make the voice very clear and pure, and the dialogs easier to understand and sharper in sound. Each speaker has an output power of 20 W, creating a total output power of 40 W, which produces good quality and very audible sound. It has preset equalizers for better sound and you can choose from heavy, clear, soft, vocal and flat equalizer modes. The radio tuner is digital and can store up to 30 FM stations and 15 AM stations as preset stations. This facilitates automatic tuning whereby you simply scan your preset channels and choose the desired or clearest frequency. The CD player supports CD, CD-R and CD-RW formatted discs and MP3 and WMA music file types. You can also play your iTunes from your iPod when it is connected. It also has bass and treble sounds controls for better sound reproduction and it has a surround sound function that resonates the sound even more in the room or at home.

Other functions

The model can be mounted on the wall and you can easily install screws so that it can hang so that you do not free up space for this new machine. When you connect your iPod or iPhone to it, it will automatically charge regardless of how long this device plays, you don't have to worry about a power outage or flat batteries. You can also use the special timer to set sleeping and reading times, which can be permanent or daily depending on your preferences.

The remote control facilitates navigation in the device considerably, even remotely. You don't have to get up and press different buttons to get what you are looking for. You also have the choice to play music from an external audio source that can be connected via the AUX connection.

conclusion

I am a very happy owner of this very compact and affordable but very powerful music maker. And because I like it, I thought you might like it too, and I've shared all the great features of this machine with you. The Panasonic SC-HC30 compact stereo system is a great addition to the home entertainment system and I wouldn't mind giving one to my mother because of the low price. You never know, you might want to get one.

Drupal - Everything you need to know about this Open Source CMS

Drupal is one of the best open source software. Drupal is specially made for the content management system (CMS) and has several unique functions that make it very different and much more powerful than its other CMS counterparts. Scripted in PHP and generated under a general public license,

Drupal has become a favorite choice of developers in recent years. Because it is free of license fees, more and more companies are choosing Drupal to build their websites and other web applications. The market share of Drupal is around five percent and confirms 2.2% of the total number of websites on the virtual platform. Although behind WordPress in terms of popularity and downloads, Drupal has built an excellent reputation as a robust tool for creating complex websites and applications. This is an open source CMS intended for business use and therefore it feeds the websites of The Economist, BBC, NBC, Mint, Arizona University, MTV UK, Amnesty International, University of Oxford and more. The story of the beginning of Drupal starts at the University of Antwerp, when students Dries Buytaert and Hans

Snijder created a joint news forum with a wireless bridge to connect with friends and share ideas, announcements and news. After graduating, Dries decided to put the software online to stay in touch with his friends. When registering the domain name, Dries thought of village.org. "Village" means "village" in Dutch. But he misunderstood "village" as "drop" and the Dries decided to keep the name. As soon as drop.org was online, the public began to grow and soon it became a community to talk about the latest web technologies and innovative ideas. Syndication, moderation and authentication systems were discussed in depth and drop.org was transformed into a space for personal experiments. It was in January 2001, Dries released the software behind drop.org as an open source project, with the name "drupal". The new open source software was therefore available to a large community of developers and can be viewed and edited by anyone. And the rest is history. More than 1,979 themes and 26,547 modules are currently available on Drupal.org. In addition, it has the world's largest community of more than one million developers, designers, strategists, editors, and other professionals working together to provide support and improve open source software Compared to WordPress and Joomla, Drupal is the most difficult but most powerful content management system. What makes the development of Drupal so unique? The benefits are numerous, including enormous scalability, free scalability, flexibility, fast implementation, first-class security functions and an affordable price. Instead of concentrating on the general market for blog platforms and portfolio websites, Drupal has bigger plans for the future. It is preparing for the business segment and in recent years Drupal has aroused a lot of interest among users of the company. Reliability, system scalability, manageability, security, interoperability and availability of resources have made Drupal an enterprise-class CMS. Moreover, the open source CMS is highly adaptable to meet all requirements of the company. The agile development methodology that is followed for Drupal development makes a rapid deployment of web applications possible. If you are

considering launching a website or e-commerce store, Drupal is an ideal choice for an open source platform to consider. But make sure you hire the most qualified developers to work on the project to benefit from the best quality solutions. As the popularity of Drupal increases, it can be difficult to find experienced and qualified Drupallers. A better understanding of the different types of Drupal professionals is an integral part. So you need to know if you need a theme, a site builder or a module developer for your project. Knowing and asking about your needs is the first step in hiring Drupal developers. Once you have found some potential candidates, it is time to deepen their experience and professional skills. Checking their work portfolio or following up on their former customers can be useful. Ask if they are members of the Drupal.org community. If yes, ask for their user number and browse their profile to view them Activities. Finally, plan a meeting with the candidate. You can discuss your needs and request their proposed work plan. If everything falls into place, you have the right professional to entrust your project.

Everything you need to know about buying wicker bar stools

Bar stools are increasingly becoming furniture in the house, which can be made from different materials and one of them is wicker bar stools. Unlike its name, they are not only used to offer seating at the bar, but wicker bar stools can also serve as decorative pieces in parts of your home where you can entertain guests to get their attention and admiration. Most wicker furniture is made entirely from rattan, a vine related to the palm tree that grows in India and Southeast Asia; although they can also be made in combination with other materials such as bamboo and wood, with its distinctive weave design. This design gives it a naturally attractive appearance, and because the materials grow abundantly in nature, they are favored as an alternative to wooden furniture, which is a good thing for those who care about the environment. Whether used indoors or outdoors, wicker furniture is lightweight and durable; two qualities that some people value this furniture more than traditional furniture. You can choose from many styles and colors, but before you go to furniture stores for your bar stool, first read the following tips about buying wicker bar stools.

1.   First, you need to know about the places where you can buy wicker furniture. Online shopping seems to be common nowadays, although shopping at furniture stores offers you the advantage of seeing the item firsthand.

1.   You may want to visit different furniture stores or websites before choosing an item that you want to buy to miss designs that may be better than what you have chosen. It is always best to limit your choices by purchasing the item that matches your preferences.

2.   Always consider color and design when buying wicker furniture or new furniture, as these must match the theme you are looking for and must match well with other existing furniture.

3. The other wicker furniture has simple designs and you can use accessories with a seat cushion for more comfort.

4. The wicker bar stools are with or without backrest. Barstools without a backrest work best in small spaces and are also easier to transport than those with a backrest, although the latter is more comfortable to use than the first.

5. Always check the skill of the item for loosening or sagging to ensure your product's ease of use. Also check the durability, because you would not want to suffer an accident with a defective bar

stool. Another thing you might want to check is whether the woven ends protrude, which can ruin your clothing if they are accidentally caught on it.

6.   Regarding the length, the average suitable for an average person is 30 centimeters long, leaving enough room to comfortably place the legs under the counter. There are also longer wicker bar stools for taller people and smaller ones for children.

The life of this writer: the cheat sheet

I am often asked where I get my ideas or how I write my poetry/texts. The truth is being told, I am not entirely sure ... a thought or feeling just comes to my mind and I will have this urge to get a pen and paper to "get out." I honestly cannot explain it; when the muse strikes, words come to my mind and I end up with a poem or words. I have to speak honestly about one thing ... I'm not just waiting for the muse to strike. If I did that, I would rarely write - or finish half a song, and the muse decided to leave me to my vices. I have what I call "cheat sheets" that I can consult when I am separated from my muse.

What is a "cheat sheet"?

A "cheat sheet" is just a notebook that I always have with me. Inspiration can come at any time, regardless of whether you can work on the idea at that time. Very often inspiration strikes at unsuitable times. It is sometimes like this that my `` cheat sheet '' is useful, I may not be able to work on the poem or lyrics right away, but I can write it down later to work. The "cheat sheet" is often useful when I come across an idea that I can work on, but I don't know how to use it. Another good use for the "cheat sheet" is to write down lines or sentences that attract my attention. I may be working on another piece and the perfect line comes to me ... just to see that it has nothing to do with my current project. I can easily save it on my "cheat sheet" to come back to it later. How often do you spend hours on a poem to get stuck on a line or verse? By taking a break and looking at your "checklist", you can find a solution to the problem or get inspired by one new writing project by leaving the problematic part. The use of a "cheat sheet" can be endless - you are only limited by your imagination.

The "cheat sheet" and the writer's block

Every writer will suffer from the dreaded writer's block at some point, so just like me, you can spend months without a single written word. I think the "cheat sheet" can help heal writers; at least to a certain extent. How on earth can you ask a 'writer' to remedy the blockade of writers? It's very simple, even if you don't have current inspiration for a writing project, you can have `` Cheat '' hundreds of ideas, rules, sentences, etc. that you have been inspired in the past. There can be dozens of poems, words or story ideas on the pages of your 'checklist'. Just start by looking at your "cheat sheet" and note down all the rules, sentences, etc. who could come to you. Otherwise, try to group some of these lines into similar themes. Once you have a collection of these thoughts on your new page, see what you have before you. Can you write something with these words? Are there other thoughts that come to mind when you look at them? Keep writing down all the ideas and thoughts that come to mind and try to structure them until writing a piece [whether it is prose, poetry, texts, etc.].

You will soon discover that you are writing again and that the block of dreaded writers has disappeared. Writing may or may not be good, I cannot make any promises in this regard, but you no longer have a blank page in front of you and you have something to show for your efforts. If it's not right, you have to keep working until it's all right.

XSP Cheat Sheet

In this article, I discuss my experience with the XSP cheat sheet. Before I tell you what I have concluded, I think it would be better if you heard about my experience with the XSP Cheat Sheet. I reason that you can draw your conclusions in this way and at the same time read my conclusions. After using XSitePro for a few weeks, I started revising the XSP cheat sheet. I can report that I thought the XSP cheat sheet was presented step by step. Many of the changes were easy to make and were not things I had learned elsewhere. However, it was the only SEO guide that was specifically designed for XSitePro and that I knew. I went ahead and implemented most of the XSP

Cheat Sheet techniques, such as file names, etc. Unfortunately, after finishing, I did not see results from the techniques I had implemented on the XSP cheat sheet. I stopped doing something else with the XSP cheat sheet and decided to focus on my pay per click campaigns. I have started redirecting my traffic generation efforts through my AdWords account, in particular by further optimizing various campaigns and advertisements. About three weeks had passed and my AdWords efforts were rewarded, as shown by the AdSense earnings I received from my websites. To further improve profits, I began to analyze the analysis of all my campaigns and websites. I discovered that after about a month, the pages I made with the XSP cheat sheet got a good traffic flow. I had never done promotional techniques on these websites. Some sites have received as much traffic as sites that have received pay-per-click traffic. By researching my statistics and tracking software for the websites in question, I found that people found my websites through the search engines - with the same keywords that I had optimized for using the magazine. XSP cheat.

Poker Cheat Sheet - Know which hands to play

You don't need a rocket scientist to understand the rules of poker. You just need to understand the basic rules of the game and know which hands you should lay during the game. This poker cheat sheet is designed to help you understand some of the most basic principles of poker in general and to help you develop your strategies. After all, a card player is not determined by the amount he pours at the table, but by the strategies he uses to win round after round.

Poker Cheat Sheet # 1: First learn the game and get to know Lingo

These days it is not enough to say that you are going to play poker. There are so many variations on this card game that it is fairly easy to get lost in the "poker talk". So for clarification, poker is poker ... except when people say video poker (which is a computer game/slot machine); and Red Dog Poker (which looks more like the game of Blackjack than anything else.) All other variations such as Five Card Draw, Omaha, Primero, Seven

Card Stud, Texas Hold'em and Three-Card Brag have the same winning principle: you have 5 cards needed to have a winning hand (hopefully!).

Poker Cheat Sheet # 2: Know when to fold and when to go with Gut Instinct

Some of the most "notorious" card players believe in 2 things: luck and their instinct. Although these seem fairly harmless, as a beginner you should not forget that poker is a gambling game; and happiness can become sour so quickly, and your feeling can only be a build-up of gas on the taco that you had for dinner. Conservative play is a way to learn from the triumphs and mistakes of other players. After all, you cannot expect that you will always win and you certainly do not always want to lose. Bet carefully at the start of the game. If you find your cards less desirable, fold immediately.

Cheat Sheet # 3: Stop trying to find out if your opponent is bluffing!

If you think your hand has a chance to fight, you can slowly raise your bets. The other card players on the table stack too much money on the table and you constantly wonder if he is bluffing or not. Instead of wasting your energy discovering the truth behind these horrible poker faces, focus on this one fact: your opponent may not be bluffing at all! And stop bluffing. This risky move (according to statistics) has only a 1% chance of winning. Poker is all or nothing. If you think your hand will win, hold it. Otherwise, it is best to go to bed while you are early.

Cheatsheet 4: know which hands to hold

The face cards are undoubtedly the best things to get because there is a chance to give a winning hand when you have a set. However, one or two or three cards mean absolutely nothing in a poker game. You need five ... always five. So instead of just focusing on face cards (which many beginners tend to do), think about the 5 cards - the hand and how it will behave in the game. A straight flush can win a full house. A street can win a hat trick.

And never forget the power of a high card hand; it can also be the only thing your opponent has against you.

The rich cheat sheet

People think you have to cheat to get ahead. Unlike Madoff, the rich have a cheat sheet that keeps them in a mentality that creates wealth and helps them attract and retain wealth. Here is the common cheat sheet of the rich:

o Have a clear picture of what you want and what you are going to do to get it. Do you have a financial goal, such as sending your children to a private school to change that next year? This type of flip-flop costs you every year. You lose your focus on what's important or you try to spread your wealth over too many desires and you to lose. The rich have a clear picture of what they want. They also know what to do to get there. Do not wait longer than you can. Do you expect your portfolio to earn 20% per year and your income to increase steadily? Well, wait. Wealthy people see their ability going up and down regularly and that doesn't upset them because they are watching the end of the game and never give up on this goal. You should do that too. Leave a legacy. Do you want money to buy luxury items and luxury houses? Most people do that. But rich people earn money to support a lifestyle they want and they build a legacy that not only supports them but also future generations. Make good choices. This is what we say to our children and this is what we must do to create wealth. Of course, we are not going to achieve several successes in succession. But by usually making the right choices, we achieve a high return. Time, money and the right choices are synonymous with real wealth.

o   Have a support team. Not everyone has family support and that's why it's so important to have the right people with the right information to help you build your financial empire. You must be the quarterback of a team of professionals such as an estate planning lawyer, an insurance broker, a financial adviser, and an accountant. They must be loyal, trusted team members who are charged and always look for your best interest. The Rich Cheat Sheet can help you focus on what you need to do to develop a wealth creation mentality to attract the wealth you deserve. On your journey to the perfect body, your diet will form the majority of your efforts. Your diet will make up around 75% of all the effort you put into! That's why it's so important to make the right decisions about your diet.Use this list as a cheat sheet to make healthier decisions. All foods play a role in your weight loss, but the ones mentioned above are of the least importance and the ones listed below are the most important.

canvas example

An overview of the art of the outer fabric.

There are different forms of outdoor art. Defining and categorizing this form of human entrepreneurship is difficult because there are no clear boundaries. Anyway, a wall painting or perhaps even a garden image can be considered as outside art. In short, people want artwork outside for aesthetic reasons. Although the goal is seemingly trivial, there are psychological explanations why people like seeing artworks in their outdoor space. When people decorate their backyard, garden or lawn, they usually have no canvas art in mind.

But the art of the canvas is increasingly being used outside. These works of art are usually found indoors to decorate otherwise boring pieces. They are a great addition to your interior as long as you choose the right one. However, it can also decorate your terrace or veranda. There are online canvas art galleries for you to find out what it looks like. The art of the outer fabric, on the other hand, can be protected from the sun by UV varnish. The varnish can also protect the canvas against bad weather, rain, and wind. Moreover, thanks to the glossy finish they are easy to maintain. You just have to wipe the surface. Canvas art is available in various types. At first glance, they look like painting on canvas, but they are pictures on canvas. Technology makes it easier now. It no longer takes weeks to finish a large canvas. It can be printed and finished within a few hours. You don't have to find a talented painter. With the shortage of talented painters now, it can be difficult to order canvas painting. And if you find one, the costs of the services are enormous. You must, therefore, be satisfied with the artworks that are available for your terrace or veranda. There are many canvas sellers online, and many of them have a wide range of artworks. The popular species are images of nature that provide a relaxed atmosphere. Beach photos are also popular. So you can probably bring the Caribbean atmosphere directly to your balcony or watch the sunset over the picturesque beach without leaving the house. These works of art are fascinating, to say the least.

When choosing art on canvas, keep the following in mind:

- Color scheme

- Design of the outdoor space

- Image

- Size of the canvas

- preference

- price

Because there are different types of art on canvas, it is wise to make a wise choice. A work of art on your outside wall should match the environment. Otherwise, the entire configuration will be strange. Keep in mind that the art of the canvas on the wall gives an illusion of space. A large beach canvas on the wall can enlarge your terrace or veranda. However, make sure you purchase a canvas photo that is suitable for your wall. It can measure 30 "x 40". This means that they have a 3,4 aspect ratio, like most images. Read the product specifications when buying canvas landscape artwork for outside online, so that you end up buying the wrong piece of outside wall art. Also, don't forget to check the shipping costs and surcharges.

How to stretch the painting on canvas

Picture Framers Use Stretcher Bars

Stretching a canvas painting is fairly easy if you follow a few simple steps. When a painting is made on a cheap canvas or other poor quality material, it is better to seek advice from a professional framework because stretching certain images is difficult and delicate. In this article, you will learn how to stretch the painting on canvas, how to choose and cut a stretcher frame, and how to complete the stretched painting so that you can hang it up to display it. Over the centuries, artists have chosen different surfaces for painting, ranging from rough plaster walls, wooden panels, paper, and fabrics. When an artist paints on fabrics, it is common to first prepare the canvas with a primer. Primer layers are very important when it comes to not only the right surface to accept paint, but also to provide sustainable support that will not deteriorate quickly. As a brief overview to help you understand the nature of a canvas painting, the steps for preparing a traditional canvas are as follow. The first step was to choose a suitable substance. Artists used linen rather than other fabrics because of the solid fiber-like construction and stability. The cotton canvas was a poor second choice when linen was not available. The fabric was traditionally coated with a layer of primer based on animal glue or pearl glue. These adhesives are made from gelatinous materials extracted from rabbit skins and other products of animal origin. The purpose of the dimensioning was to cover each strand of the fabric with a layer that, once dry, would seal and protect the fabric. The second step was to make a mixture of rabbit skin glue mixed with dead plaster and whiting or chalk. Dead plaster is made by stirring the plaster of Paris for about half an hour with water. When you mix plaster beyond the curing time, you change the crystal structure, so that it does not dry out and cure like traditional plaster, so dead plaster. Dead gypsum has a different structure than that of whiting added to the glue to make the artist's gesso. The heated mixture of glue,

whiting and dead plaster was then applied to the surface of the preformed fabric. Different layers are applied in successive and alternating layers, creating a smooth, serrated surface that accepts paint. The trick to applying gesso was to apply a layer and then wait until it loses its glossy appearance before applying the next layer. The canvas was dried after several layers.

1.   Artists often made this preparation for the fabric after it was stretched over a support frame.

2.   The fabric was first stretched over a tapered rod called a stretcher.

3.   When stretching tables, it is important to choose a suitable stretcher bar with a raised lip or a tapered profile.

4.   If you simply use a flat piece of wood for your stretcher frame, painting problems will arise later by causing a print line where the wood touches the back of the image.

5.   Modern artists often buy pre-produced canvases and artist paintings with a synthetic gesso coating on their surface. It is even acceptable from conservation to use synthetic polyester fabrics instead of linen or canvas.

These synthetic fabrics are more stable and durable than some organic fabrics.

6.   A major problem concerns developing countries where artists cannot obtain quality media. I often come across paintings made on cotton sheets, jute bags, and tarps. They each present different challenges when they try to make them presentable.

7.   In short, to stretch a canvas that has already been painted, it is necessary to determine whether the fasteners or staples that you are going to use first go to the side or back of the stretcher.

8.   The process of stretching a canvas involves cutting and joining certain lengths of stretchers into a frame, or buying pre-cut stretcher pieces from an art store.

9.   The split corners consist of a sliding nail connection that allows you to stretch the canvas further after stretching it on the bars. There are different methods to make adjustable angles so that extra tension can be exerted on the fabric by widening the angles.

NOTE: If you use different stretcher bars, make sure you have this square before you stretch your canvas, otherwise the paint will deform. Measure the diagonals to check the squares. If the frame is parallel and the diagonal is equal, it is square.

1.   The paint is then placed on the frame of the stretcher, with the lip or the tapered side of the stretcher touching the rear of the canvas.

2.   You then gradually work from the center to the corners with the help of a stapler or small push pins as you pull the canvas.

3.   The trick is to work gradually on the opposite and then adjacent sides and place only a few pins at a time.

4.   Stretch tongs are a handy set for stretch work. They consist of a wide pair of pliers with a toothed handle or a rubber band to grip the canvas. They are used to pull the canvas around the stretcher bar and exert tension while you staple or staple the canvas on the frame.

5.   Sometimes staples or drawing pins are on the back if you want to see the sides of the painting without placing an outer frame on it.

6.   When you reach the corners, carefully fold the corners with a Monroe corner where the two sides overlap a central tab that is not attached. The reason is that if you want to tighten the canvas, the corner must allow some expansion of the canvas, otherwise, it will tear.

7.   You will usually have to frame the paint or at least apply a dust cover to a foam plate or other covering. The coating is important in the long term to prevent dust from accumulating on the back of the paint, which in turn retains moisture and eventually forms.

8.   You can then attach D-rings and wire to hang the paint.

9.   Professional framers prefer to frame the canvases in such a way that they are not exposed to the edges. They also like to place

the hanger on the outer frame instead of on the stretcher, because hanging the stretcher can cause an arc that causes the paint to wave.

10.   I hope this article has emphasized the requirements and techniques you can choose when stretching your paintings.

Canvas print online - an overview

The basic principles of online canvas printing

In our modern age, there is a wide range of methods available for printing photos. Gone are the days when we could only take a photo and have it developed at Boots. You can now become your professional photographer by adding effects, styles, patterns and even words in a great online canvas printing experience that gives you total control over every step of the process.

Simple canvas print online

Online printing on canvas is fast, easy and remarkably cheap. The high quality of the materials used does not lead to excessive prices, and you will see how easy it is to turn your best photos into beautifully impactful canvas art with a few clicks of a button. The canvas prints make fantastic gift ideas for your loved ones or as a treat for you, so what are you waiting for? Unleash your creativity and imagination by designing works of art that you can produce in a modern, contemporary and incredibly elegant way. Make large, large or mini canvas prints - it's up to you! The most important thing is to ensure that your photos are special to you and that they have a clearly defined subject.

Believe in the power of your photos

You don't have to be a professional photographer and you don't even have to have experience with photography - you just need a little creativity to add an extra finishing touch to your photos to enhance them just that little bit more. Choose carefully, because with online canvas prints your final prints will stay with you for years and years and may be passed on from generation to generation. You can be assured of exceptional quality, which means that your images will inspire every viewer. A great and unique addition to any interior, sparkle and a burst of color to any room in your home.

Print your photos on canvas

This process allows you to design and create truly remarkable works of art on the wall that everyone who sees them will envy. Imagine organizing a dinner at your home amid a dramatic canvas print of your family's trip to the Great Wall of China, or perhaps your parents' golden wedding! I'm sure you have hundreds of ideas in mind about how you can turn those photos you've locked into your computer into beautiful gift ideas, so what are you waiting for?

Design space FAQ

Frequently asked questions about Design Space

Advantages and usability of frequently asked questions when designing websites.

Frequently asked question pages (frequently asked questions) are an underestimated option in the website design process. Frequently asked question pages are one of the most important pages a website can have. It is at this stage that a visitor indicates that he is interested and what his objectives are to visit the site. Users are interested in the products or services of the website. If designed correctly, the page can attract visitors' attention and improve the conversion rate. The frequently asked questions appeared in 1982. When advanced with email functionality, news, visual designs, and analysis help visitors easily find the information they want. The frequently asked question pages also save time and money by answering most questions regarding products and services by e-mail or customer conversation.

Advantages of frequently asked questions

The best alternative to search: although a search can serve the same purpose as a page with frequently asked questions, most search engines do not work so well. The search terms of the visitor (verbal alternatives) may not match those of the website's vocabulary. This can become more complicated if the search query specified by the visitor is insufficient. Quick links are used to facilitate bad search results. The frequently asked question is a better option than quick links because it provides a background and perspective for research, rather than just a list of links. It offers space and space to discuss interesting topics. Business advantage: frequently asked questions provide additional support for the website by providing customers with the desired information without contacting the company. It shows how easy the company is to work. Customer requests and concerns are handled before the money is spent, demonstrating that the company understands customer needs effectively. The FAQ pages increase customer confidence by providing a forum that answers their questions. The forum illustrates the passion of the organization for its range of products/services and the willingness of the company to communicate with potential buyers. The FAQ pages help save the organization's time and working hours that would otherwise be spent on managing and responding to customer questions. The FAQ page improves the SEO evaluation: the content of the FAQ receives a positive SEO evaluation because it is indexed by search engines. The Key Efficiency Index assesses the number of searches or a particular terminology and its completion. Expressions or keywords with a high KEI have a high volume and little competition. SEO for a website can be improved by identifying and placing the right questions that a

website can answer. Search terms or searches formulated as questions have a better index for keyword effectiveness. The questions and answers on the FAQ pages must be aimed at the right target group and must be relevant. The SEO rating of the website can be considerably increased by directing the user to pages with relevant content. Help with navigation: the well-developed FAQ pages contain interesting and useful topics that must be designed to look visually clear and understandable. The design of the information in the frequently asked questions helps visitors to browse through the desired content and find additional information. The trusted quotient contributes to the user interface: web designers focus on improving the design of the page by adding interesting widgets and tools to the website. The technique of user interface design is to make these widgets intuitive for users. A frequently asked questions page is the simplest and best known of all tools to make the interface intuitive for a new visitor, so descriptive and standard labeling of questions must be done.

Usability - Design an effective page with frequently asked questions

1.   Users need a FAQ page. Questions from users or comments received on the website can help to track questions on the FAQ page.

2.   Immediate repetitive questions that customers ask by phone help to understand the pattern of questioning potential customers. This can serve as a basic framework for designing questions.

3.   A clear starting point for the frequently asked questions page - in the main navigation bar or the footer (or both) must be visually distinguished from the rest of the webpage. This is different from other information. In general, visitors consult the menu at the top and bottom of the page to search for important links. The answers to each FAQ

question must be linked at the top for long FAQ pages.

4.   The content of the frequently asked questions page should be easy to read with contrasting colors for the text and background, with well-spaced lines and letters with good CSS typography (color, size, font, decoration, etc.).

5.   The questions and answers must differ from each other. Different fonts or background colors can be used.

6.   Questions must be classified intuitively to avoid confusion. Categories have short descriptions and are arranged hierarchically in order of importance.

7.   It is very important to include the search function for long FAQ pages. It is difficult for users to browse through all questions before

they find the desired question. For categories, a search query can be added if different categories and subcategories are involved.

8. The role of images in the artistic appeal cannot be denied. The use of pictograms that support different categories can increase visual appeal.

Frequently asked questions are an important way to attract the right group of people to your website and provide a forum where people can communicate with the company. They can serve the strategic interests of the company if they contain good content and are well structured. A user experience researcher must analyze user questions and comments to help route information to the organization in a planned manner.

Be prepared - 10 questions that your interior designer can ask you

The most important element of a successful interior project is a good plan. As your interior decorator in Seattle will explain to you, there are many aspects of a project to consider, such as the judicious use of space, the good creation of atmosphere and the creation of a room. visually pleasing. Bringing everything together is a challenge, to say the least. To successfully reach this point, a good interior designer will ask many questions before developing a plan for a project. As a customer, you must be prepared to answer these questions. Your job is to reach the ultimate goal of this beautifully designed space of your dreams. Ask yourself the following question:

1. How do I usually use this space? Will it be a space for activity, relaxation, work or perhaps a studio? Consider how it will usually be used.

2. What other use would I like to include in this space? If secondary applications are planned for this component, also indicate this. Areas for different applications must be built into the plan from the outset.

3. Will it be a high-traffic area, and if so, how can I imagine people moving around in this space? Study the location of this space to determine if it can be used the way you want without interrupting the natural circulation of

your global space. The design of a seating area with a solarium that is only accessible to the main bedroom may not be ideal if you intend to use the room for entertainment.

4.   Will the overall plan also include other parts? If you ultimately want the project to contain changes to other parts, these changes must be defined at the beginning, even if the actual work has to be done at a later time.

5.   What type of lighting do I need or need in this room? Do I need bright lights for games and activity, warm and subtle light for quiet moments, or maybe some?

6.   Do I need additional mechanical components, such as electricity, heating or plumbing? These aspects are usually expensive and in some cases structurally

impossible to install. It is better to know from the start whether this is the case.

7.   Do I need special noise reduction or noise improvement in the design? For example, for a home theater, you can consider using materials that offer better sound quality.

8.   Do I want and is it possible to add extra windows or doors? You may want a window to enjoy beautiful sunsets, but the room must fit in.

9.   What kind of feeling do I want the room to have? This is where the color of paint, fabrics, and textiles can be used in various ways to create the perfect atmosphere for the room.

10.   What is my total budget for the project? It's easy to get carried away when creating a dream space. Know your limit and stick to it

Chapter 4

TIPS FOR SOLVING THE CRICUT DESIGN SPACE

Tips for solving Cricut design problems - come back to designs! Do you have problems with Cricut Design Space?

Does it charge slowly, does it freeze completely, does it crash or does it not open at all? It is so frustrating when it happens because you just want to continue with your project, right?

I know what it does and in this article, I'm going to give you some tips on what to do about these design space issues.

Troubleshooting Cricut design space

1.   Slow internet connection

The main cause of problems with Design Space is a slow internet connection. The program requires good and consistent download and upload speeds. Inconsistent connection to the valleys and tips can also cause problems for the software. You will probably get a more consistent connection if your device is closer to your modem. Sites such as YouTube require good download speeds and you can make ends meet with lower download speed. But Cricut Design Space requires good to download and upload speeds because you constantly send and receive information when you work on your design.

Perform a speed test

Perform an internet speed test with a service such as Ookla.

Cricut specifies the following requirements for the correct functioning of Design Space:

Broadband connection

The minimum download of 2 to 3 Mbps The minimum download of 1 to 2 Mbps

Contact your internet provider if your results are very bad and you think this is causing or contributing to your problems. You may need a new modem to deliver the required speeds. It was my problem a year or two ago. A new modem completely solved my problems - it's just hard to wait a few days!

2. Your computer

If it is not your internet speed, the problem may be the computer, tablet, or mobile device that you are using. There are recommended minimum requirements for the correct functioning of Design Space. Here are the basic principles:

Windows computers

Your Windows computer must:

run on Windows 8 or higher

have an Intel Core or AMD processor - mine has AMD and works great have 4 GB RAM

a minimum of 50 MB of free disk space - the better, the better have a free USB port or Bluetooth connectio

Apple computers

Your Mac computer needs the following to make Design Space work: Mac OS X 10.12 or something new

1,8 a 1.83 GHz processor have 4 GB RAM

Have 50 MB of free space

an available USB port or Bluetooth capabilities

Background program

Another issue may be related to too many background programs that run when you try to use Design Space.

Do you watch Netflix, chat on Facebook, skype your mother, upload the last season of Fixer Upper, upload your latest Vlog to YouTube and try to design a t-shirt in Design Space? Well, in addition to earning a medal for doing it at the same time, you'll have to close a few programs to make DS work properly.

But seriously, that can be the problem, even if you don't do this all. Sometimes closing things that you don't use speeds up.

Other things that can help

Here are some other things you want to test or add

clear your cache and history

check what your antivirus software is doing and update if necessary Bijwerken updated drivers (for Windows)

defragment your hard drive Malware Perform malware check

These tests help speed up your computer or can all solve the problem together.

3.   Your browser

10.   Your browser can also be the cause of problems with your design space.

11.   Cricut indicates that you must use the latest version of a specific browser. Whether you use Chrome, Mozilla, Firefox or Edge, make sure it is up-to-date.

12.   If one browser does not work, check if it works in another. Sometimes, for unknown reasons, this can solve the problem.

CHAPTER 5

HOW TO WORK WITH IMAGES, TEXT, AND COLORS

Work together with your web designer

You have now decided to create a new website. All our congratulations! Now the work starts. In this article, you will find some things that you want to take into account when your website comes to life. A web designer advises you to use a domain name that brings at least one good keyword to your website. The web designer helps you with suggestions for obtaining a good domain name. Most customers have already taken this step themselves, sometimes with success. First, it is very important to know why a website is needed. There must be an explanation of what the site is for and what visitors can get out of it. This helps the web designer to plan an appropriate overview of how the website can be broken down and changed over time as needed. It is, therefore, the best plan to maintain a long-term objective.

Earrings with enamel pencils and chalk

Artisans have used clay throughout history to make jewelry. From the most primitive cultures, through ancient Egypt and the Ming dynasties to the present, clay has been used to enhance the fashion of the day in the form of rings, pearls and other decorative items. Ceramic earrings have become an everyday fashion accessory in our culture. They are easy to make and decorate with enamel pencils, crayons, etc. Here's how to start: Cover the table surface with a layer of newspaper and apply a thin slice of clay to it. By rolling on the newspaper instead of on the canvas, you get a fine surface of smooth clay instead of the woven surface of the canvas. Use another piece of newspaper on top of the clay plate to prevent the rolling pin from sticking to it. You can place plugs on both sides of the clay so that the plate reaches a uniform thickness of approximately 1/8 inch. The surface of the clay can be textured with blocks, households or found objects, even toys. The type of press for children can be used to place text on the clay surface, because the type is already reversed, which gives a positive image on the clay. Almost any textured surface can be used to create patterns: paint tray coverings, tree bark, embossed wallpaper, floor mats, edited buttons, etc. they all offer striking results. The only limit is that of the scale: the earrings are small, each design on it must be small enough to be seen. When pressing objects on the clay, care must also be taken that the clay in the sunken parts of the image is not too thin. If the glazed chalk is to be used in the final decoration, the stripes must not be so narrow that the chalk does not fill them. Images can be layered or merged to create more depth and variation. If a matching pair of earrings is desired, a double print must be made for the second earring in the pair. Once the plate is full of duplicate images and textures, it's time to find the earrings underneath. Look critically at the most interesting and visually appealing impressions. Imagine how the image can be cut into a definitive shape, such as an earring. Maybe the round silhouettes work better; maybe diamonds; or triangles; or narrow rectangles. The cropped or cropped image must be aesthetically balanced and attractive.

Cut out the first earring with a knife; then find a second earring in the images that match or are complementary to the first earring. Place the first earring on the plate and follow the shape of the earring with the knife to cut the matching earring off the plate. While the first earring is still stacked on its double stack, make a hole with a needle at the top of the earrings for the wire loop. Keep cutting pairs of earrings off the plate; set them aside until they are as hard as leather. Then smooth the edges of the earrings with a damp sponge to remove the sharp edges and burrs. Let the clay dry completely and fry the earrings in bisque. The glaze can be used to define and accentuate the images in relief by first glazing the entire surface with a sub-glaze, such as the brushstroke, and then rubbing the dried glaze from the high points with a kitchen scourer. Remove any dust from the earrings with a damp sponge. Now the earrings can be pulled. Cooking with raku carbonizes the bare clay into the black during reduction after cooking. With oxidized firing, the bare clay remains white. If you want to add another color, you can carefully brush the glaze on the upper parts. This produces color in the negative parts of the design. The glaze can also be painted by hand on individual parts of the design for extra emphasis or contrast. Make sure to glaze the front of the earrings so that they do not melt into the oven rack before baking. Hooks for earrings can be made from any hypoallergenic thread specially designed for earrings. Eye pins and hooks can be ordered online from many jewelry suppliers.

Give your customers image-based search engines

The power of visuals

Often repeated yet true, "an image says more than a thousand words" correctly indicates the power of visual images in the e-commerce industry. As more and more retailers develop new strategies to connect with customers on a wide range of portable devices, visual search engines are presented as the next big thing. In the e-commerce space, visual search reads images to identify color, shape and size and even text to identify brand and product names. Such research offers a major advantage over keyword research, where the search results are only as good as the user's ability to describe an item. The impatient buyer who wants to make a quick purchase and wants to go further takes a long time to describe the details or characteristics of a product. In this rapidly changing world, is it not more convenient for the customer to simply take a photo, upload it to the image-based search engine and let the engine do the work?

The algorithm behind image-based research

1.   How does image-based search technology work? An image search engine that is meant to search for an image, the search can be based on keywords, an image or a link to an image. Content-based image recovery or CBIR, as it is called, contains vision techniques to identify images based on colors, shapes, and proportions. The results depend on search criteria such as metadata, image components or the search technique used by the browse.

2.   The search for images by classification is based on the comparison of metadata linked to the image in the form of keywords, tags, text or description and is obtained in the form of a series of images sorted by relevance. The

metadata associated with each image can refer to

the image title, format, resolution, color, etc. However, such a survey method does not always produce accurate results.

3.   On the other hand, image search offers search results, for example, by comparing images using a clustering technique. The research groups bundle images of similar content and investigate various aspects of the image, such as color, shape or texture, making it a more efficient and reliable method.

Characteristics of image-based search engines.

Image-based search engines are offered by various software companies with which e-commerce giants can offer a truly enjoyable user experience. Some of the solutions offered using tools such as JAVA, Monody, OpenVMS, Python, HTML, JavaScript, WCF include

- Web portal and mobile application with integrated visual search technology

- Segmentation of computer vision

- Algorithms for sorting and classifying images

- Machine learning algorithms

- Application integration with an image search algorithm

- Performance optimization

The benefits of image-driven search

To enhance the online shopping experience and encourage order conversion, online retailers and e- commerce website owners are now integrating efficient image-based search engines. With image- based search engines, retailers can:

1.   Increase the overall shopping experience: the normal online customer is often bombarded with thousands of articles and visuals on e-commerce websites. Many times the customer likes a product but is pressed on time to make the purchase. When the customer returns to the website to make the purchase, they invariably have to perform countless unnecessary searches on their

laptop to find the product they had previously seen and liked. With visual search technology, buyers can easily take a simple photo of their desired product and search for the product in the image search engine to retrieve the exact product, significantly reducing browsing time and increasing overall shopping experience.

2.   Respond quickly to customer questions: With millions of items sold on e-commerce websites, online retailers have difficulty responding quickly to customer questions. Search methods for existing products. forces users to search for products manually, which is not only time- consuming but also annoying and unproductive shopping. By automating the search process with CBIR, customers can now find the products they want to buy by simply uploading an image.

Give customers more options

Image-based search engines help empower customers, allowing them to bridge the gap between addiction and buying. This technology offers an unprecedented level of usability, allowing faster search results, greater accuracy of results and thus a more rewarding e-commerce experience for your customers. Read more about image-based search engines and their applications here.

imagine

The psychology of the imagination

About how imagination helps us survive, create, escape ... from reality.

Okay, this way of discussion can become very interesting if we explore the limits of the limitless mind. When it comes to imagination, forget the brain and focus completely on the mind. This does not mean that the brain plays no role in the imagination. On the contrary, the brain plays an important role, but for purposes of human preference, the imagination in this discussion remains the mysterious phenomenon hidden and created deep within the layers of the mind. The duality of mind and brain, suggesting that mind and brain are separate entities, remains a philosophical problem, but we appreciate this duality when we try to explain phenomena, such as imagination. So close your eyes and imagine yourself being transported to this unreal world, distant land of angels unknown to humanity, and a variety of food, drink, and fruit that you never thought existed, or in a country full of technological miracles, unthinkable gadgets and invisible in the human world. What have you seen now? Yes, the imagination helps us to see or live beyond what our senses allow us. Imagination stretches our mind and it is our mental exercise. Imagination drives us to new areas and helps us to explore the unnatural and unusual. Now close your eyes again and think that you have brought this new type of gadget back to earth. It is something that people have never seen or heard. What does this gadget look like? These are imaginative exercises and as your schedule for the gym, if you close your eyes for 15 minutes every day and propose something new - a new design, a new building, the new car, you will probably be very surprised at how much the mind can stretch and discover or invent new things. It is the power of imagination and imagination is a very powerful tool. Imagination is the basis of new ideas and creativity and helps an artist to create magic on canvas and inspires the writer to weave dreams into his story. Imagination is about stretching your mind beyond its limits and the more you do it, the better. It is a kind of exercise for the mind and helps to improve creativity enormously. The imagination brings mental and emotional flexibility and makes the personality more open-minded and adventurous. People with a strong imagination more often take emotional and social risks and are less calculated. They are generally more brave and adventurous. Some may like the escape of the imagination and try to stay immersed in a fantasy world to overcome suffering and stress in real life. For example, the imagination can make a person adventurous and open-minded, but after a certain level, the imagination that becomes a continuous fantasy can affect mental health and push the individual to escape so that he separates himself from reality. Staying immersed in a fantasy world is bad for a person's mental health. So here too we need a balanced imagination. Too much of something is always harmful. The imagination that leads

to pathological fantasy leads to psychological problems. On the one hand, there is the good side of imagination, creativity, the acquisition of new ideas and knowledge, the improvement of the adventure and the flexible openness of life. On the other hand, imagination can lead to excess, fantasy, escape and associated vices such as drugs, alcoholism, and mental illness. Creative individuals and geniuses who can stretch their minds have a high imagination. Similarly, drug addicts or the mentally ill also have a very high imagination. In the case of a creative genius, the imagination is more constructive and positive, and in the case of the addict, his imagination is destructive and negative. Your imagination can make you a genius, a great writer, a painter or a scientist because scientists also need a lot of imagination. Your imagination can be an addict, an escaped person and a person who wants to stay in his fantasy world with alcohol or mood-enhancing drugs. We need to know how the imagination works. Why do we introduce ourselves? The reason we imagine is that we must escape reality and need the inspiration to survive. Imagination is like a mood-enhancing medicine and makes us feel better. Once we begin an exercise in imagination, it can become addictive and the imagination has the power to control the mind. For example, think of your mind like a ship and your imagination as powerful waves. It can take you anywhere and let you perish or it can help you navigate and discover. to estimate. The mind must always keep control and help keep the imagination in balance. To respond to how we can imagine, the physiology of brain mechanisms during the imagination must be studied further to provide insight into the imagination process. The 'why' and the 'how' lead us to the question 'what' do we imagine? Our imagination usually corresponds to our wishes and preferences. If we desire something, we imagine it and in the imagination, we satisfy some of our possessions. Whether you like it or not, the imagination can drive you crazy and the imagination also makes you healthy. If we can't get something and feel depressed and terrible, we like to think we have that object and we feel much better. The imagination gives us our natural placebo and we find pleasure on the run. Video games and mobile games are important to some people because these games integrate imagination and desire. It allows escape such as drugs, such as alcohol, such as sex, and that is why we are always safe even in this extremely stressful world because we have escape routes. Without imagination, we would not have progressed as a race and we would not have survived as a society. A healthy imagination shows us the future we want to go to, gives us a purpose and we live for a reason. Imagination shapes our dreams and ambitions and gives us the power to overcome setbacks so that we can turn our fantasies into reality. Now imagine a completely different kind of ice cream that nobody has ever had before and also imagine that you now have a scoop of ice cream when you read this. So are you feeling better?

Imagination is the mother of knowledge

It is said that necessity is the mother of the invention. Every invention also leads to the creation of new knowledge. Thus knowledge is created to satisfy the needs of people. How does human necessity or desire become knowledge? The answer lies in the ability of people to imagine what lies beyond sensual perception It is through human imagination that all knowledge has been created. Knowledge can be represented in any form, such as words, images, a diagram or an audiovisual medium. Knowledge of knowledge once again arouses the imagination as needs evolve, which again provides new knowledge.

What is unimaginative knowledge?

Knowledge has no meaning without imagination. Imagine reading the scriptures for a dog. It certainly cannot affect the dog. Imagine giving a book in English to someone who doesn't know English. It makes no sense because he cannot understand it. Even free images of the language barrier only affect if they can lead to a person's imagination. The image of the most beautiful women in the world on an animal would not affect in the same way that the most important physical patterns are useless for a man of art.

How are we so certain that we will answer the above questions even without reading the text for a dog and measuring its response?

The answer is again "imagination".

We don't seem to know the answers to most questions by reading books or by experience, but purely by imagination What we consider to be knowledge is nothing but imagination that is set in motion in the mind of the knower of knowledge. The knowledge that does not appeal to the imagination has no meaning. Even words like love, God, intelligence are nothing but the knowledge that arouses the imagination of something in us. This imagination can vary with each person, but they all have common imaginative qualities. Every knowledge is nothing but a word that has a lot of imagination. For example, if we say "The Theory of Relativity," it activates the entire relativity theory (if we understand it) that can be explained on many pages. If someone knows the theory of relativity, these words have no fantasy and no meaning. If you say the word, like Bill Clinton, "it means a person with so many attributes. You can spend your entire life explaining what it means to be God, Love or Bill Clinton, including the aspects that you create from your imagination that the world is still unknown to.

Scientific knowledge and imagination

Scientific knowledge is often considered factual and unimaginative. However, this does not seem to be true. Consider the theory of the atom. The Bohr atom model states that each atom consists of a positively charged nucleus with protons and neutrons surrounded by negatively charged electrons. So when we think of the atom, the image of the atom is represented by our mind like all planets that revolve around the sun. However, some information about the atom is not yet known. For example, how the positive proton came together to form a nucleus that overcame the repulsive force against the same charges. That is why the neutron was born and integrated into the core. Where the electrons came from and started turning around the core. These are inexplicable facts of atomic theory because they are currently beyond human perception. Consider one of the first theories about physics, namely. The gravity discovered by Newton. We know that all material bodies experience an attraction for each other. We have precisely measured the quantum of this force and its relationship to mass and distance. Yet we do not know how this power works? Scientists previously thought that there is something called a gravitational wave that is present between masses, although such a wave has never been found. With his general theory of relativity, Einstein explained that the result of the acceleration of the mass is the same as gravity. This means that if you are in a confined space such as the lift, you cannot see whether the force you feel is due to the gravity of a mass or the acceleration of the lift. When Einstein gave this theory of the space-time continuum, it was not easily accepted because other people could not imagine what Einstein had thought by making the theory of relativity. Consequently, his theory went unnoticed for more than 15 years. Many of these theories die of natural death because people cannot imagine the content of these theories. The same applies to the other frequently observed forces that exist between electrical charges and magnetic substances. All waves of electrical and magnetic charges are imaginary but useful to understand the effect of charge or magnetism. By pursuing your imagination, you can easily conclude that even assuming that gravitational waves, electric charges, and magnetism exist, it still cannot explain how waves cause attraction or repulsion. This aspect always surpasses the imagination of man, therefore outside the field of scientific knowledge. Now consider the Big Bang theory. This explains many things that we know about the universe, except that it is impossible to know what existed before the Big Bang. There must be something that existed before the Big Bang, but no theory is created because it is beyond the imagination of the human mind.

CHAPTER 6

Printing and cutting

Reduce distribution center costs by printing and applying labels

Budgeting in a distribution center is important, as is reducing costs without watering down the value or image of the distributed product. For this reason, new handling solutions have become efficient and efficient a popular way to take every distribution center to a higher level. By reducing labor, training and product costs, these automated systems bring manual techniques back to the Stone Age.

Stay competitive with automated label printing and application systems

Automated processing systems in one step, such as light sampling and printing and applying label systems, ensure maximum reliability for delivery to every center. Most distribution centers around the world have adopted this software and used it as part of their management systems. That said, it is crucial to stay one step ahead of the competition and keep up with the competition. The loss of customers due to the lack of integration of a newer and more profitable material handling system can lead to a decrease in profit margins and a loss of activity in return.

Keep your warehouse organized and on course

When it comes to business simplicity and efficiency, the use of an automated program can reduce the work of company employees by half. The system itself is easy to understand and easy to train for every employee. By having the training time with the latest technology, money can be saved in the short and long term. Employees will be sure that they easily use the latest technology.When a company is ready for an upgrade, different solutions are available. When it comes to picking to light, send pick pack and print and apply labels, some options can meet the exact needs of every company. Upgrades are just as easy to use and understand as the original automated systems, which mean there is less downtime in your warehouse and more products at the door.

Do it all in one simple step

Label printing and application systems are a management solution for each existing label and multiple barcode printing equipment. In one step, the machine can scan new or existing bar codes and print and apply labels and packing slips accordingly. The program also checks shipping labels and delivery notes, bringing it one step closer to employees and further reducing labor costs. With a speed of one thousand five hundred units per hour, it seems almost astonishing that a program can work so consistently and efficiently.When comparing label printing and the application system with that of a manual system, up to 15 manual programs are required to do the work of one automated system. And the hardware costs of an automated machine are about half that of manual machines. By reducing labor costs, labor restrictions, training time, material costs, distribution time and more,

it is easy to see how a company can effectively reduce distribution costs using a print and application label system.

Increase productivity with print and application label systems

Label printing and application systems save time and money for distribution centers through warehouse automation. The technology also increases sales and productivity to record levels. Some centers unknowingly think that setting up and installing such a product would be long and tedious. Contrary to this belief, the installation and configuration of any project that uses labeling and application labeling systems, such as that of a pick nick ship, takes only a few moments.There are many benefits to using up-to-date warehouse automation equipment, including increased productivity and capacity to distribute even more products to your customers at lowers costs.

Save time and money with printing and applying labeling equipment

This technology is so advanced that it can reduce the workflow of any label project in one step. By simply applying packaging and shipping labels to products that are distributed outside of your center, this warehouse automation equipment has a proven track record of handling more than 25 boxes per minute with exact consistency and precision. This means that 1500 boxes per hour and 12,000 boxes per eight hours of work can be distributed by your team,If consistency and accuracy are not sufficient, the system can also reduce the number of employees needed to complete a project manually. This, in turn, saves money on your activities for inaccurate working hours and the extra employees that would have been needed every day without the advanced label printing and application technology.

Discover the precision of every project and every profession

Communicate directly with the WMS or shipping system that your warehouse already has, the print and application label system creates shipping labels and packing lists immediately after scanning the code to existing package bars. Validate, monitor and manage every product for you and your team, this technology is truly a one-step process that is accurate every time.

It is important to increase accuracy to preserve existing businesses and also to get quality references for new businesses later.

Why limit the number of customers you could have by not using the best and most advanced technology for warehouse automation on the market?

Combination of Pick Pack Ship with printing and labeling systems

By narrowing down the workload of your employees one easy to understand and complete step (pick, pack, ship) your center becomes an expert distribution almost immediately. Combining picking software technology with the print and apply label system, your warehouse automation distribution operation is on its way to cutting cost and truly performing at an optimal level of service. You can also utilize other technologies with pick-pack-ship and print and apply label systems. The option is endless once this technology is put into place. So what are you waiting for? A simple solution to increased profit, decreased costs and a better customer service experience for client is at the fingertip of any distribution center ready and willing to succeed.

CHAPTER 7

MAINTENANCE

3 Keys to a Successful Preventive Maintenance Program

1. Careful Planning of the Preventive Maintenance Program

• Select a planning and accountability system (preventative maintenance software, CMMS software or equivalent)

A good list of preventive maintenance tasks contains the following components:

- Equipment.

- Tasks.

- The person to whom the task has been assigned.

- A task interval.

- Start date and expiration date.

- Optional: detailed instructions and photos if required.

- Optional: a sequence of tasks.

Start with your equipment list. If possible, then collect the correct tasks for the preventive maintenance task lists from the

OEM manuals or online manuals. It is a good starting point, especially with newer equipment. In some cases, the equipment warranty depends on compliance with OEM recommendations. Another source of tasks is the experience and intuition of the

maintenance manager. Another source is sites that use similar equipment. When developing a task list, consider the reusability of task descriptions. Reusability refers to the use of the same job description on possibly multiple devices. The advantage is that there are fewer tasks, no duplicate task descriptions, and better PM reports and analyses. Consider these examples:

Description of the task REUSABLE: lubricate the roller chains

NOT REUSABLE: Lubricate the roller chain on conveyor # 1

In the first example, this task, lubricating roller chains, is suitable for all equipment that is equipped with a roller chain. In the second example, lubricating the roller chain on conveyor # 1 is only suitable in the PM task list of conveyor # 1. Imagine how hard your efforts to manage preventive maintenance software will be if you do not use reusable tasks. Another example that can cause problems later is naming conventions such as 30-day PM or weekly tasks. This causes unnecessary redundancy because the interval is already included in the PM record. Moreover, no task description refers to the work performed. How do you make reusable tasks? Start with the most generic tasks you can think of and create them first. Examples can be Inspection, Cleaning, Lubrication, etc. After these task descriptions have been made, go to the next step and create slightly more specific tasks. Here are some examples: Check the wiring, replace the lubricant, the lubrication chains. Continue with more and more specific tasks, always trying to prevent you from including the equipment or component of equipment in the task description. Finally, for specialized tasks that are only performed on specific equipment, it may be necessary to include a part of the equipment in the description of the task. Keep the task description short and focused on the actual task. It is clear that if the description of the task is short, it may not fully describe the work. Detailed instructions and images are used here. Then determine which interval units are required for your PM system. PM recorded on a calendar usually used days. For example, every 7 days Lubricate the roller chains. Other tasks can be described on request or based on the actual autonomy of the equipment. In some cases, hours or minutes may apply. As you gain experience with this set of PM tasks and intervals, changes in tasks and intervals may be required. Therefore, choose a system that makes editing existing PMs easy and without losing historical data.

Make sure the right resources are available

Here are the resources you need to complete a preventive maintenance program:

- Trained and available staff.

- Sufficient spare parts, consumables, lubricants, drive chains, bearings, etc.

- Time in the production or execution schedule of the equipment to perform the PM.

- A motivated team of maintenance professionals.

Personnel must be trained and able to perform the required work safely. Apply the correct lockout / Tagout procedures vigorously. The available inventory for consumables and other spare parts used for PM must be sufficient.

Inadequate spare parts not only prevent the completion of PMs but also influence motivation when employees trying to use their work are hampered by the lack of spare

parts. As such, the purchasing department must have an ordering system that precedes the need for spare parts for preventive maintenance. Also, a responsibility system (CMMS) follows the use of spare parts for replenishment purposes. In short, show your maintenance technicians how important you think preventive maintenance is for the equipment and training needed for these important tasks. Time is a resource. The staff must have time to do their job. This may require planning changes so that maintenance personnel are available during planned equipment outages. With the right resources, your maintenance team can only be motivated to successfully maintain the equipment.

Use maintenance software to track and manage maintenance

Now that tasks, intervals, personnel, training, and planning have been determined, it is time to load the data into a preventive maintenance software system. With so many CMMS choices, it is important to do your research carefully. About fifty CMMS companies stop their activities every year and fifty others replace them. Choose a reputable, long-term CMMS company that has proven itself. When choosing a CMMS, ask the following questions:

- How long has the CMMS company been active

- How flexible is the preventive maintenance system

- Are there different formats for task lists

- Is it possible to automate the transfer of the task list

- Can technicians close their PMs while maintaining data integrity

- Is it possible to close the PM without leaving the factory floor

- Is it easy (or difficult) to adjust the schedules for preventive maintenance tasks

- Are labor and parts costs easy to summarize and report

- Is there an objective way to know how to optimize task lists or task intervals based on downtime or reliability data

When evaluating a CMMS it is best to perform a demo copy of the proposed system with your equipment and tasks. Use the system for at least 30 days. Send lists of preventive maintenance tasks to your staff. Get their membership by demonstrating the usefulness of the system. Show yourself and your service technicians that using the software makes your job easier. In particular, confirm that this system can improve the availability and reliability of equipment.Consider support and training as part of the initial investment. Training in CMMS software is certainly worth the investment because it enables the maintenance department to quickly become familiar with CMMS and give confidence in its use. This leads to better compliance when entering and updating data. Price is important, but the actual cost-benefit of CMMS does not come from the initial investment in CMMS, but from continued use and the benefits that result from it. Some CMMS software solutions are subscription-based. Others are a one-time investment with a perpetual license. Although there are several factors to be taken into account when selecting CMMS, initial investment (price) should have a low priority when the budget allows it. Ask yourself the following question: "Do you want to rely on a cheap CMMS for millions of dollars in assets?"

2. Implement your new preventive maintenance program

This is the time to reap the benefits of your new preventive maintenance program. Here are some questions that you should take into account when implementing your new PM program:

- Should task lists be printed, sent by e-mail or easily viewed via a tablet or smartphone

- How are tasks completed and what information must be included

- Who must perform preventive maintenance tasks once they have been completed

- How are you going to use the system without maintenance personnel

- Should the spare parts lists be included in the task list

- If spare parts are included in the task list, should the inventory levels automatically decrease when the PM is completed

The answers to these questions come down to company policy, industry requirements, regulations, and personal preferences.

Evaluate and adjust the maintenance schedule of your equipment

The constant evaluation of your preventive maintenance program is an integral part of the effective management of this system. Equipment schemes change, equipment demand changes, personnel changes, maintenance technologies, and procedures change. The maintenance data of the equipment is your most important assessment tool. The longer you use your CMMS system, the more data it collects. Assuming you have chosen a CMMS that offers detailed analysis and reporting, this data is now valuable decision storage. Use this data for OEE (overall equipment efficiency) and reliability analysis. Choose a CMMS that uses MTBF (average time between failures) to suggest intervals for preventive maintenance tasks. The use of actual execution data to define PM task intervals eliminates the guesswork. As a proactive maintenance manager, you must adapt to these changes if necessary. Here are some things to watch out for and some ideas about how to respond. Bear in mind that sometimes there is no substitute for the intuition of an experienced maintenance manager.

Changes to the equipment implementation schedule

In some situations, preventive maintenance can only be performed if the equipment is in planned downtime. This causes a problem for maintenance planning. Here are some ways to deal with this situation.

- Operators of maintenance-free machines can perform certain simple maintenance procedures, such as minor lubrication work.

- Double equips certain equipment when it is off.

- Adjust the maintenance schedules.

- Use automated maintenance devices, such as grease nipples.

- Implement preventive maintenance procedures during unforeseen downtime.

Changes in equipment request

The demand for equipment is not limited to changes in the schedule. The demand reflects the actual operating time of the equipment and the amount of work it performs during the planned period. It is clear that in these cases it is not useful to activate PM based on calendar days. In this case, it is best to activate PM based on the operating hours, cycles, malfunctions or the correct meter unit for this equipment. This equipment must, therefore, have a counter or be connected to the system that automatically triggers preventive maintenance orders via an OPC-compliant data connection.Select a CMMS software solution that reads OPC data directly from the equipment and then automatically responds at the right time with a preventive maintenance command.

Staff changes

The best way to overcome this inevitable change is to have detailed lists of preventive maintenance tasks, intervals, spare part requirements, and history. Ensure that this information is available to pass on to the new person. The clearer your system, the easier it is to follow this change transparently. Again, good software for preventive maintenance meets this need. Besides, ongoing training and cross-training in various maintenance processes can compensate for staff change issues.

Changes in maintenance technologies and procedures

An example of this type of change could be a new sensor that delivers critical maintenance data to an OPC server. These data, in turn, indicate the correct PM interval. Another example can be simple to operate the equipment only when needed. This promotion saves energy resources and can reduce equipment wear. The software is constantly being improved. The desired options with software solutions for preventive maintenance are:

- Is there a role-based authorization capacity with which maintenance technicians can close their PM?

- Is there a mechanism for validating closed PMs by technicians?

- Is there the possibility of temporarily assigning tasks to another maintenance technician?

- Is it possible to collect performance data via an OPC-compatible data network and automatically issue work orders?

Overview

Preventive maintenance is one of the most important responsibilities of the maintenance manager in a production environment. Many activities of the maintenance department are influenced by and depend on a successful preventive maintenance program. Most importantly, the success of the entire plant is directly proportional to the quality of the design, implementation, and management of the preventive maintenance system.

CHAPTER 8

BEGINNER PROJECTS TO BE IMPLEMENTED

Woodturning Delights - Projects for beginners and gift box

One of the things that surprise many wood turners is the expression of wonder on the face of those who see the objects that even a novice wood turner can make. This, coupled with the need for the beginner to develop new skills, provides a secondary but great joy in woodturning, building the wood turner's gift box. Beginners have a few choices in methods for developing woodturning skills, exercises, and projects. Of course, this list is neither complete nor final but works well for all purposes. The exercises encourage the learning of cuts, positions, and results through repetitive work on the wood that turns into curls and kindling wood. Although it has its place in the training of all wood turners, it can be a boring process after a short period. Projects for beginners are called this because they are easy to implement because they generally require little wood and cut and require basic procedures. At the same time, they make it possible to learn basic skills that are useful in later and more complicated procedures. The nature of the projects means that they are most useful if the same company is repeated several times, with the intention that each company is better than the previous one, which indicates a learning curve.The advantage of project-based learning is that it has a series of finite objects that can be compared to determine the learning curve and see points for improvement. Moreover, there is the satisfaction of having several useful and decorative items. This can also be a problem in some cases, but with a great solution. Take the modest candlestick, for example. It can be a great beginner project that includes the work of the spindle and the faceplate as well as the assembly and gluing process. He also learns how to turn straight lines, pearls and inlets, the standards of the wood-spinning repertoire. Once you are ten, twenty or fifty years old, the first or two seem suitable for the ignition box, while the others are more than ready to be exposed. The question may then be, what do we do with fifty or even twenty candlesticks? A great answer is the wood turner's gift box, a place to store most of these duplicates for friends and family who admire the manufacturer's hand touch. It is satisfying to give a gift that first gave the donor a pleasure and a pleasure to learn, which is difficult to measure. For many wood turners, the pleasure of creating an object is only matched by the pleasure of giving it to someone who appreciates the finished work. The art and handiwork of woodturning contribute to the pleasure of giving and the satisfaction of seeing a work well received and used. Darrell Felt mate is a wood turner whose website, Around the Woods, contains detailed information about woodturning for the novice or experienced turner, as well as a collection of wood turners for your enjoyment. You too can learn to turn wood, here is the starting point. Wondering what it looks like? There are many free videos on the site about everything from grinding to making a bowl. There are various woodturning projects fully explained on the website. In particular, a selection of projects for beginners can be found on the Projects for Beginners page with step-by-step explanations and photos.

Projects for beginners Woodworking - Woodworking as a hobby

One of the most important things to keep in mind when you start woodworking is that it is a hobby. It must be fun as a hobby. Whatever you choose for your projects, woodworking must be something that you enjoy and not something that you see as work. There are many things you can do to ensure that you continue to work with wood as a fun hobby.

Choose sensible carpentry projects

When you start, it can be easy to get discouraged by the lack of projects at the beginner level. Don't be put off by the plans. Do your research instead. Find a project that is at your level, but also those interests you. In the beginning, you may have to undertake projects that seem a bit boring, but these projects teach you the skills you need to execute the most advanced projects.See your beginner projects as a woodworking lesson. You must leave these projects after you have learned something new. If you have not learned anything, it may be time to go to a higher level of difficulty.Once you have completed projects for beginners, carpentry projects can be more about your passion. Start choosing projects that you are passionate about. Choose projects that give you a complete article that you can be proud of and use. This helps keep your passion for the hobby alive.

Work when you have time

Do not force yourself to complete projects. Woodworking is something that can be done bit by bit. Maybe you only have twenty minutes in one day. Let yourself relax for twenty minutes by doing a little bit about your project, Then come back to work on another day.

When you get the feeling that you have to work with wood, it starts to feel more like a chore or obligation than a fun pastime. Don't let yourself work. If you don't feel like working on your carpentry project, don't do it. There is always another day.

Watch out for financial tensions

Woodworking can become expensive. However, keep in mind the costs to make your finances easier. Make plans to use the equipment that you already have. Use scrap wood. Do what you can with what you have and buy new equipment and supplies when you have the money.

Consider buying second hand or even borrowing what you need. It is not necessary to turn your hobby into an edition that you cannot afford.

Don't stand on your carpentry projects

Remember that this is all a hobby. You must always have fun with your projects. Woodworking should relieve stress, not the cause of stress. You must feel relaxed when you carry out a project. If you are not, you may need a break. Never let your hobby change into something that you are afraid of. Ultimately, your projects, your carpentry hobby, and all experience must be something you enjoy.

Affiliate X review: the good, the bad and the ugly

Don't buy Affiliate Project X yet unless you don't mind losing your shirt.

In recent weeks there has been a lot of hype about the X affiliate project Chris McNeeney has done an excellent job of raising the product and introducing people to many daring claims. He also includes many killer techniques in his Affiliate Project X guide, but there is a big mistake that underlies his entire book. He forgot a lot of details.What many people don't realize is that these omitted details are crucial to success in the neighborhood of that promised by Affiliate Project X. Very few people are willing to take a book with advanced techniques and start running with it. There are many experiences that must be gained by trial and error. Nothing is worth it. I would not recommend buying Affiliate Project X if you buy it because of the sales page. The Affiliate Project X does not keep its promises on the sales page. If you are already a successful internet marketer, it is quite possible that you can adjust your methods with the advice in Affiliate Project X to increase your profit. However, if you are just starting out, Project X hardly offers you what you need to succeed.What newcomers to internet marketing should take seriously are private membership sites that offer mentoring. There are a handful and others arrive every day. A beginner can benefit greatly from personal coaching and mentoring of those who have already passed. Internet marketing has a very long learning curve and without the right support structure many people are lost, frustrated and ultimately abandoned.However, the internet marketing experience can be much more fun with the right support structure, first and foremost a supportive learning environment where you are constantly aware of your efforts and encouraged to stay consistent.

Astral projection for beginners - 3 hours until your first OBE

One of the most difficult and frustrating parts to get involved in the OBE experience is the difficulty that most people experience to have a meaningful experience to support their spiritual journey. As a dedicated practitioner for more than a decade, I spent a lot of time writing on astral projection for beginners, because we were all one in the beginning! In my experience, the key to having a successful projection is very simple: you have to change your conscious state into a state that lends itself to experience. Let's see what I mean As every discoverer of the hardcore in the frontier of consciousness will tell you, the human mind is a wild and woolly instrument, hard to tame by the conscious will. Many Zen practitioners will call it "the ghost of the monkey" or "the ghost of the mirror" and for those of us who are interested in the experience outside the body, we can certainly confirm that the will to project is not enough to be there to come. The easiest way to leave your body is undoubtedly the use of hemispheric brain technology that will "train your brain" to reach peak states of altered consciousness. Simply put, this technology takes over the way your mind jumps, jumps and moves from place to place while you work on the mechanics of a projection. By soothing the mind and letting the smooth surfboard of technology take you, you will find yourself surfing through the supernatural realms in no time! Remember that brain training technology has been used for more than 25 years to cause conditions outside the body has been tested by many scientific communities, including some of the world's most famous transpersonal psychologists. It is a proven way to open your mind and your world to potentials that 99% of the population will not even consider, let alone explore!

Five reasons to repeat woodturning projects

Although each piece of woodturning is a project, the term is more commonly used to describe a planned piece of woodturning produced and described by others. It must now be transformed into another store by another person and of course, the result will also be slightly different. Here are five reasons why wood turner searches and runs different projects. First of all, they are educational for the wood turner who wants to learn or develop techniques. It is relatively easy to choose projects that are at the top of a person's woodturning skill or even a little further. Although the rotation of an element is starting to teach the new skill, most projects are completed quickly and the rotation of several will reinforce the new knowledge. Secondly, repetition increases the depth of knowledge of a certain skill. Woodturning is more than physical or intellectual activity. Instead, it incorporates aspects of both. What the mind determines and what the eye sees must be done by the hands. Repeating a project reinforces certain cutbacks in certain situations. The same situations usually appear in future projects once they are learned because the mind now has data to search for and the hands can perform them. Thirdly, old knowledge is brought forward and the gymnast remembers past skills under simple and safe circumstances. Although the gymnast's repertoire contains only three parts; straight, handle and pearl; There are many ways to cut and with a varied selection of tools. The techniques must be practiced and with the help of designated projects, the practice can yield useful and welcome results. Fourth, one of the skills that all wood turners must develop is the ability to saw accurately quickly. By turning pieces in duplicate, you can take the time to measure and go to the measurement to carefully match the first piece with the second. Although this is, of course, important with chair pins and the like, it is also necessary for a set of salad bowls or candlesticks. By repeatedly working on measurement, the eye can gradually make sufficient cuts in an environment that moves just as much as wood. Fifthly, turning double pieces provides a better understanding of the wood that we have chosen. Wood moves with temperature and humidity. Two wooden pieces that can even come from the same tree and even less of the same species will be executed slightly differently when they are sitting and dry. Although this is clear from two different pieces, it is even clearer from two pieces that resemble each other as much as possible. In other words, photographing a series of duplicate works offers a better understanding of the art and crafts of woodturning. At the same time, the challenges provide a lot of pleasure in learning itself, This is the win-win situation of a wood turner.